CULTURAL POLITICS

Pre-Raphaelites re-viewed

CULTURAL POLITICS
general editors Jonathan Dollimore and Alan Sinfield

Writing Ireland: colonialism, nationalism and culture
David Cairns and Shaun Richards

Poetry, language and politics   *John Barrell*

The Shakespeare myth   *Graham Holderness*

Garden—nature—language   *Simon Pugh*

Opera, ideology and film   *Jeremy Tambling*

Teaching women: Feminism and English studies   *Ann Thompson and Helen Wilcox (editors)*

Race, gender, Renaissance drama   *Ania Loomba*

Pre-Raphaelites re-viewed   *Marcia Pointon (editor)*

Pre-Raphaelites
re-viewed

edited by Marcia Pointon

MANCHESTER UNIVERSITY PRESS
MANCHESTER and NEW YORK

distributed exclusively in the USA and Canada by ST. MARTIN'S PRESS

Copyright © Manchester University Press 1989

Whilst copyright in the volume as a whole is vested in Manchester University Press,
copyright in individual chapters belongs to their respective authors, and no chapter may be
reproduced wholly or in part without the express permission in writing of both author and
publisher.

Published by Manchester University Press,
Oxford Road, Manchester M13 9PL, UK
and Room 400, 175 Fifth Avenue,
New York, NY 10010, USA
Distributed exclusively in the USA and Canada
by St. Martin's Press, Inc.,
175 Fifth Avenue, New York, NY 10010, USA

Reprinted 1990

British Library cataloguing in publication data
Pre-Raphaelites reviewed. – (Cultural politics)
 1. English paintings. Pre-Raphaelitism –
 Catalogues
 I. Pointon, Marcia, 1943–
 II. Series
 759.2

Library of Congress cataloging in publication data applied for

ISBN 0–7190–2821–3 paperback

Photoset in Linotron Joanna by
Northern Photototypesetting Co, Bolton

Printed in Great Britain
by Bell & Bain Limited, Glasgow

Contents

Illustrations

Foreword: Cultural politics

The break-up of consensus in British political life during the 1970s was accompanied by the break-up of traditional assumptions about the values and goals of literary culture. Initially at specialised conferences and in committed journals, but increasingly in the mainstream of intellectual life, literary texts have been related to the new and challenging discourses of Marxism, feminism, structuralism, psychoanalysis and poststructuralism, and juxtaposed with work not customarily accorded literary or artistic standing.

Some recent developments offer a significant alternative to traditional practice; others are little more than realignments of familiar positions. But our belief is that a combination of historical and cultural context, theoretical method, political commitment and textual analysis offers the strongest challenge and has already contributed substantial work. We call this *cultural materialism*.

There are (at least) two ways of using the word 'culture'. The evaluative use has been more common when we are thinking about 'the arts' and 'literature': to be 'cultured' is to be the possessor of superior values and a refined sensibility, both of which are manifested through a positive and fulfilling engagement with 'good' literature, art, music and so on. The analytic one is used in the social sciences and especially anthropology: it seeks to describe the whole system of significations by which a society or a section of it understands itself and its relations with the world. Cultural materialism draws upon the latter, analytic sense, and therefore studies 'high' culture alongside work in popular culture, in other media and from subordinated groups.

'Materialism' is opposed to 'idealism': it insists that culture does not (cannot) transcend the material forces and relations of production. Culture is not simply a reflection of the economic and political system, but nor can it be independent of it. Cultural materialism therefore sees texts as inseparable from the conditions of their production and reception in history; and as involved, necessarily in the making of cultural meanings which are always, finally, political meanings. Hence the series title: Cultural Politics.

Finally, cultural materialism does not pretend to political neutrality. It does not, like much established literary criticism, attempt to mystify its perspective as the natural or obvious interpretation of an allegedly given textual fact. On the contrary, it registers its commitment to the transformation of a social order that exploits people on grounds of race, gender, sexuality and class.

The Cultural Politics Series seeks to develop this kind of understanding in a sequence of volumes that has intellectual coherence, but no restrictive format. The books will be both introductory and innovatory: introductory in that they will be clear and accessible; innovatory in their application of distinctive perspectives both to established topics and to new ones. In the tradition of Shelley, Arnold, Eliot, the Leavises and Williams, though often in terms very different from theirs, culture and politics are again at the centre of important intellectual debates.

Jonathan Dollimore
Alan Sinfield
University of Sussex

Introduction

Have you noticed, my boy, that the painting here is based on Homer, or have you failed to do so because you are lost in wonder as to how in the world the fire could live in the midst of the water? Well then, let us try to get at the meaning of it. Turn your eyes away from the painting itself so as to look only at the events on which it is based. Surely you are familiar with the passage in the Iliad where . . .
Philostratus, *Imagines*, I.i

The celebrated passage from Philostratus's *Imagines* has been invoked frequently in debates about the superiority of verbal over visual communication (the *Paragone* debate) and in support of the capacity of visual imagery to produce a forgetful state of wonderment. This passage, written some 1,300 years before the group of artists who called themselves the Pre-Raphaelite Brotherhood met in London in 1848, suggests that some, at least, of our current theoretical preoccupations are not new. The competing claims of texts underpins Philostratus's question to his pupil. Yet that question: 'surely you are familiar . . .' is a false one. Historicism may recover for us conventions and mediations obliterated by time, familiarity with Homer might help in this process. But the major question – that of how diverse texts relate – is not posed.

This collection is informed by that question of intertextuality, the question of how the specific historical experience, formed as part of the processes of political, cultural and sexual power, intersects with other (earlier) texts (verbal or visual), also themselves ideologically formed. In this book we argue that it is necessary to examine the text at its point of cultural production and to insist that Pre-Raphaelitism is not seen in isolation from other pictorial practices if we are to understand the way in which ideology is constructed across fields rather than within them. It is not merely that we are dealing with painters who also wrote. Nor is it simply a matter of taking another look at a group of artists who turned to specific periods in history. The questions of style and of history that are familiar landmarks in Pre-Raphaelite literature are not ideologically neutral. They encode particular ways of representing the world.

In re-viewing Pre-Raphaelitism the authors of this book entered a field characterised by an international and prolific literature. The Brotherhood were enthusiastic letter-writers and their relatives (brothers and sons for the most part) saw it as their duty to establish the reputations of these artists in print. The 'life and letters' model, established as a dominant mode by the artist's immediate descendants, continues to hold sway. Diana Holman Hunt's *My grandfather, his wives and loves* (1969) has recently been reprinted (1987). The papers of the 'circle's' members are also appearing in print. *The diaries of George Price Boyce*, edited by Virginia Surtees (1980) and *A Pre-Raphaelite friendship: the correspondence of William Holman Hunt and John Lucas Tupper*, edited by a group (Coombs *et al.*) and published in 1986 are recent examples in this genre.

The 'artists and their circle' model, of which Raleigh Trevelyan's *A Pre-Raphaelite circle* (1978) is a typical example, lends itself particularly to collecting and exhibiting. One or two 'authentic' Pre-Raphaelite works can be offered for display, supported by material from the 'circle', thus offering an appearance of coherence that may or may not bear historical investigation. Thus, for instance, in 1978 the Australian National Gallery in Melbourne published *The Pre-Raphaelites and their circle in the National Gallery of Victoria, Melbourne*. In the same year the first edition of the catalogue of the Bancroft collection in the Delaware Museum appeared, recording and documenting the contents of this remarkable but not atypical collection of a Quaker mill-owner in the early years of the century: Rossetti's *Found* and Hunt's *Isabella and the pot of basil* are in company with drawings and paintings by Pre-Raphaelite acquaintance, manuscripts and photographs (Delaware). The fact that the circle has grown ever wider may, beneficially, have something to do with a scholarly concern with historical contexts or may, less beneficially, be connected with the purchasing of papers by American archives and the writing of theses.

The 1960s rediscovery of the Pre-Raphaelites has reached its apogee in the 1980s. Landmarks have been the invaluable cataloguing work of Mary Bennett (Bennett, 1965, 1969) and Virginia Surtees (Surtees, 1971), and the publication of *The journal of Pre-Raphaelite studies* which began life as *The Pre-Raphaelite review* in 1977. The 1984 Tate Gallery exhibition was particularly noteworthy. More of this later. But perhaps the most significant events – and ones which mark a general level of cultural acceptance of a group of artists whom, I recall vividly, were thought risible in the token lecture delivered on the subject of Rossetti as poet and painter when I was an undergraduate in 1965 – have been the return of Manchester City Art Galleries' splendid nineteenth-century rooms to their original state, complete with aspidistras and Morris, Marshall & Faulkner Co. furnishings, and the Open University Arts foundation film on James Leathart, the Pre-Raphaelite patron from Newcastle upon Tyne (1987).

This general approbation for, and promotion of, a body of art and the ever-widening definitions of Pre-Raphaelitism should make us pause for thought, occurring as they do in a decade dominated by calls for a return to Victorian values and a market for Laura Ashley interiors. As Lynda Nead points out, it would be easy to suggest a straightforward revival of 'Victorian values' in the 1980s. Nevertheless there are striking resemblances 'between the representations of sexuality in the Victorian period and the organization of sexual behaviour in the present . . .' (Nead, 1988, p. 10). We might add that, in terms of historiography, Pre-Raphaelitism offers a clear case of nationalist, nostalgic, 'Little England' ideology. Through the close intimacy of the 'circle' as defined in literary and historical description, a paradigm is offered for art that is at one and the same time titillating in its revelation of the individual life and non-threatening in its closure. Indeed the political implications of a major Pre-Raphaelite exhibition in London in 1984, sponsored by Pearson, Inc., did not go unnoticed. It was pointed out that the dates 1961 and 1984 served as a frame of reference. 'The former marks the beginning of a massive appreciation in the value of Pre-Raphaelite works as commodities on the art market. The latter celebrates the rising status of the works in academic practice with a full scale curatorial and art historical ratification' (Cherry and Pollock, Dec. 1984, p. 481). Cherry and Pollock then mention the involvement of Pearson in cultural production through the communications and leisure industries it owns implying a continuous linking chain, though what this might mean is not explored. Our task, in looking again in detail at the Pre-Raphaelites, is to pose questions of cultural politics that will challenge and explore the bases of the market and entertainment definitions of Pre-Raphaelitism identified at the time of the 1984 exhibition.

The idea of dream as an escapist antidote to the horrors of industrial Britain was a popular theme in the 1960s and formed the basis for much writing about the Pre-Raphaelites (e.g. Cecil, Spalding). It has continued as a powerful international currency. In 1981 *Els Pre-Rafaelites a Catalunya: una literatura i uns simbols* appeared (Cerda i Surroca) with chapters on Rossetti and William Morris headed 'polaritzacions essencials' and 'el cavallier realitzador del somni' respectively ('essential polarisations' and 'the man who realized dreams'), and in 1984 a German study of the Pre-Raphaelites was published entitled *Wie ein goldener traum* ('like a golden dream') (Lottes). The relationship between actuality and dream as artistic conventions, fantasy as discourse and the role of fairy-story in the construction of an account of the present, questions which are explored in this collection (particularly in Chapters 4, 7 and 8), are seldom if ever addressed in this strand of writing. Indeed, typically, dream is either simply presented as the condition of these extraordinary men or else a crude polarity is established between the 'real' world and the fantasy world in which artists operate. Thus, for John Weeks, introducing *The dream weavers . . .*, a collection of short stories (1980), the point is that 'these are stories of strange beauty by men of strange genius, the nine-teenth-century Pre-Raphaelites, painters who were also poets who were also sculptors and designers and craftsmen' (p. 7).

More often than not the dream proposition is no more than an excuse for talking about faces, and particularly women's faces. Jan Marsh's attempts to recuperate for the canon the lives of the women with whom the Pre-Raphaelite Brothers were associated – as wives, lovers and models (Marsh, 1985) – is a rearguard action that has served to produce an alternative but equally biographical account. Whether intentionally or not, it has served to reinforce the emphasis on the female face as a sign for Pre-Raphaelite male creativity (Cherry and Pollock). Andrea Rose's intro-duction to *Pre-Raphaelite portraits* (1981) typifies the presentation of the Pre-Raphaelites as avant garde rebels whose rebellion fulfilled a universal dream:

> [The Pre-Raphaelites] set fire to time-honoured ideas of what art was and what an artist should be. From the ashes of their assault, however, rose a bird of a rather different feather from any they might have envisaged. For the head of the body of the Pre-Raphaelites fashioned a new face – intense, iconic, wasting with unnamed passion. (Rose, pp. 4–5)

Our book is innovative and original not in the agenda it addresses – we do not claim sole rights to the discussion of Protestantism, portraiture or photography in Pre-Raphaelite production – but in the way it deals with that agenda and in what it has to say about issues which, rightly, have come to be seen as important ones for nineteenth-century studies. Questions concerning social and domestic spaces and their political articulation, concerning gender and race, representation and ideology, have been acknowledged in the pages of publications like the *History workshop journal* and, to a lesser extent in *Victorian studies*. But such work often has adopted a literal and commonsensical view of visual represen-tation, interpreting paintings and engravings (and to a lesser extent verbal texts) as illustrative of an ideology that is constructed elsewhere. We might cite as a case for the presentation of that agenda a recently published work by Susan B. Casteras which is, in fact, an expanded version of her 1982 Yale exhibition catalogue (Casteras, 1982). Casteras addresses questions such as courtship, marriage and other social themes in an account which ranges across products of Queen Victoria's reign generally and includes within its exposition major Pre-Raphaelite material. In *Images of Victorian womanhood* (Casteras, 1987) we read that 'painters *seized on the slightest pretexts* to depict amorous involvements – from railway carriages, to church pews, tearful farewells, theater balconies, and boating scenes', from 'calf love' to 'geriatric têtes à tête'. We are told that 'literary sources dominated a major classification of this genre ranging from illustrations to *execrable Keepsake verse* to Shakespearian lines or texts from the Bible. . . .' Casteras speaks of the Victorians as zealous and obsessive, matching their zeal with 'impressive statistics in the realm of fine art'. By the 1840s 'interest in courtship subjects per se *had been sparked*' and 'by the 1870s until the close of the century the Royal Academy was *virtually engulfed* with images of courtship, with captive cupids and the like giving way to essentially bourgeois or middle-class trysts'. The quality of such works varied wildly, we are told, '*from heart-rending masterpieces to mawkish or inane potboilers*' (Casteras, 1987, p. 85, my italics).

The style of this writing, like that of Rose in the passage quoted earlier, serves to reinforce prejudices about the quaint and, at least potentially, humorous nature of Victorian society. Nor is it by any means uncommon in the field. The notion of the plenitude of Victorian life (from 'calf love' to 'geriatric têtes a tête') based on a token view of Dickensian variety pervades such writing and seriously undermines its pretensions to historical exegesis. The concept of 'Victorian' enshrined in the book's title where, admittedly, it might be construed as a period marker, infiltrates the passage resulting in generalisations and elisions. Who are these Victorians with their zeal? Impressive statistics are a device that the British government of today has effectively inherited from the nineteenth century. Here the phrase appears as transparent truth, as unmediated fact. Painters are presented here as individuals driven by unknown forces seizing on pretexts and possessed by obsessions which are common to all of them, whoever they are. We are never told, though later in the chapter we are given some select examples.

The contributors to *Pre-Raphaelites re-viewed*, on the other hand, examine how texts relate to each other, whether they be paintings, verbal texts, institutional proceedings or events. It is in the public domain that these works ultimately signify and it is as products of that domain that they must be deconstructed. For Casteras the 'exercrable Keepsake' serves as a foil, a point of reference against which quality can be measured, though how that is to be done is taken for granted. Barlow, in Chapter 4 of this collection, on the other hand, examines how the imagery of Keepsakes functioned in relation to Pre-Raphaelite High Art Imagery, seeing how the one informs the other in a continuous axis of signification around the figure of the fantasised female. Again literary sources are listed by Casteras as generic types, whereas the authors of this collection tease out the interconnections between the verbal and the visual, never presuming that the Bible or Keats is, or can be, a source in any simple sense. For Flint, reading is to be understood as an act with social, historical and theoretical consequences. For Johnson, likewise, a comparison of Watts and Rossetti can be dealt with systematically, tracing similarities and differences across a range of pictorial practices avant garde and traditional, thus deconstructing this simple opposition.

Casteras's method is to invoke fragmentary references from primary documents like books on etiquette, without systematic selection. Once identified, these features are then matched with the subject-matter of paintings. No attempt is made to examine etiquette as social system or the book on etiquette as a genre with its own conventions. Nor is it asked who read these books or how they were used. The connection between 'women in real life' and representation of women in pictorial imagery is simply unproblematic for Casteras. It is a legacy, a given. It is precisely because the state of research in this period does not permit one surely to specify what were the 'hundreds of depictions' to which Casteras has referred that examination of pictorial imagery and cultural politics concentrates on the particular case study explored in depth. It is only by building up our knowledge of the interface between social regulation and pictorial representation that we can avoid these pitfalls. Thus marriage, it is argued in this book, is both a powerful regulative practice and a symbolic trace that underpins discourses of gender and creativity.

In case it be thought that I have unreasonably picked upon an atypical study, I will reinforce the points made above by reference to the introduction to another recent work also, like Casteras's book, from a University imprint. Tupper's diaries, we are told in the introduction to the collection of his and Holman Hunt's correspondence, 'suggest that the ideas that later coalesced in the Pre-Raphaelite Brotherhood may have been abroad long before and were just waiting for a catalyst' (Coombs *et al.*, p. 4). The authors of *Pre-Raphaelites re-viewed* do not subscribe to the view that ideas are abroad waiting for a catalyst, like chemical particles waiting for a chemist to turn them into a compound that can be conveniently identified and named. Ideas are generated within specific cultural and political conditions and are inscribed across textual representation.

It is because ideas do not simply 'coalesce' that we address questions of mediation, examining the circulation of meanings within and between discourses.

The unknown or little acknowledged text (such as the Keepsake, the drawing or the photograph) is not adduced in a supportive or illustrative role in this book. Nor is it proposed as a foil to some higher form under discussion. For we are less interested in the hierarchy that insists upon major works of art as opposed to 'potboilers' (though many of the texts we are addressing come into the accepted category of major artworks) than in society's competing interests and the claims for status and dominance of those interests in the visual and verbal fields: photography over painting, medieval over modern, the face over the body, the verbal over the visual, English over Arab. The legitimation of a field – whether it be that of a detailed 'truth to nature' style by Holman Hunt in *The awakening conscience* or the paintings of bridesmaids by J. E. Millais – is accounted for in this book not by reference to artists' obsessions or pretexts nor to a sweeping state of affairs which somehow imagery unproblematically illustrates, but within the fabric of nineteenth-century ideology.

The authors of *Pre-Raphaelites re-viewed* acknowledge their debt to the painstaking and scholarly activities of the documenters of Pre-Raphaelitism; in particular they recognise that without the 1984 exhibition at the Tate Gallery, their book would have been unlikely if not impossible. It was here, and in its aftermath, that it became apparent that questions, particularly questions about content and representation – about meaning, as Philostratus would put it – in relation to what was hung in the exhibition and what was excluded, began to be posed with some urgency. Most notably a review by Cherry and Pollock and an article in *Art history* (Cherry and Pollock, June and Dec. 1984) produced a radical agenda for an examination of the Pre-Raphaelite Brotherhood. That agenda (as Marcus suggests in this book) was provocative but impossible to accomplish. Lynda Nead's article of the same year (Nead, 1984) was a foretaste of her recently published book (Nead, 1988). Dealing with the role of visual culture in the categorisation of female sexuality in nineteenth-century Britain, this book offers a history of culture and class. Whilst it came too late for the authors of these essays, we recognise Nead's work as an important point of reference. It is also likely that Griselda Pollock's forthcoming essay on Rossetti's *Bocca Bocciata*, in a collection of essays entitled *Vision and difference*, will contribute to the still small, but nonetheless growing, body of scholarship dealing with questions of representation among this prominent group of nineteenth-century artists.

Intellectually rigorous studies of this kind are, however, the exception rather than the rule. Whilst the 1984 exhibition offered us, like Philostratus's pupil, great opportunity to gaze in wonder at a range of Pre-Raphaelite work never before or since assembled, the catalogue and the book published to accompany the exhibition (*The Pre-Raphaelites* and Parris) signally failed to explore questions of meaning. How these works signified at their point of production, what their subject-matter (literary often, though not Homeric) connoted, how they might be 'read', were questions barely touched upon. And, apart from the above-mentioned studies, they have had precious little airing since. This collection redresses the balance, including major essays on three founder-members of the Pre-Raphaelite Brotherhood and on Burne-Jones. Whilst each essay constitutes an independent unit, the concern with recurrent and intersecting discourses makes of the collection a discursive whole. With perhaps one exception, the authors are concerned less with the painting as material object (few of us devote any time to the justly celebrated question of Pre-Raphaelite colour and handling) than with how imagery in Pre-Raphaelite art signifies historically not as an act of regulation and terrorisation but as a complex and at times contradictory practice, the consequences of which cannot be assimilated into an a priori framework based on a simple concept of power or of hegemony.

The traditional concerns of art history with individual, and, above all, with masculine creativity, have been forcefully challenged during the past decade. As far as the Pre-Raphaelite Brotherhood is concerned, the production of a dominant and all-embracing art-historical account that perpetually reinscribes the patriarchal was identified by Cherry and Pollock (Dec. 1984, p. 494). The art-historical approach predicated upon the notion of the group or the circle and discussed earlier, especially in relation to cataloguing and exhibiting practices, does not propose an alternative to this account. Indeed, the Pre-Raphaelites and their circle model depend upon an unquestioned acceptance of individual male creativity which, by some form of osmosis, colours the work of the associates and lends them distinction and identity. That identity is always seen to be formed within the work of the individual, whether it be Millais or Rossetti; the process of 'influence' is itself unexamined. Thus it is possible, for example, to tack Elizabeth Siddall or Marie Spartali onto the group as honorary male artists. Only Cherry questioned, in the 1984 exhibition, what it might mean to be a female artist working with Pre-Raphaelite imagery (The Pre-Raphaelites, no. 198). The names of individual 'associates' like George Price Boyce are valorised as individuals worthy of a place in the patriarchal assembly of Pre-Raphaelitism by virtue of an *association* which is defined primarily, or more often exclusively, in terms of anecdote.

The concept of the group has thus been used to elide difference, to reinforce the dominant notion of artistic creativity, and to obscure histo= rically specific issues. It is as though, in the historiography of nineteenth-century British art, Blake, Turner and Constable can stand up to scrutiny, not perhaps on a par with Michelangelo, but at least according to the same criteria. But the Pre-Raphaelites, not sufficiently distinguished individually (and, anyway, oddly and eccentrically 'Victorian'), could be brought into the canon by virtue of the idea of the group. This concept of the group or the circle is singular and monolithic and stands analogously to that of the individual.

It is our contention that, given this state of affairs, the interrogation of the individual work can be a radical act, that to break down the homoge-nous notion of the group we must look again at individual artists and particular works. We do not aim 'to know' the artist through the work, but we do not disclaim the relevance of notions of creativity as one historical factor among many, all of which are open to examination. In this book the *idea* of a 'movement' is acknowledged as symptomatic, for such an idea functions powerfully historically. But if the *idea* of a move-ment in artistic practice is taken seriously this is not to endorse a mono-lithic and unifying linking of style and purpose.

The field of Pre-Raphaelitism as historiographically defined is there-fore our chosen place of intervention, for here our critique may be most effective. It is our aim to map a terrain of artistic production at particular moments, taking account of ideology and, in particular, grounding our work in theories of vision, spectatorship and intertextuality. Our model is that of a concatenation of texts strung out, often untidily, across time, class and nation. The rationale for choice of text is determined not by biography but by the presence of competing discourses inscribed in sites that are historically and socially specific: vision and stereoscopy, the Orient, gender, for example. We have avoided seeking the issue or event in the public sphere that might seem to encapsulate the political moment, reading off against this the texts of Pre-Raphaelite artists as social documents. Rather, we have taken some of those texts which will be most familiar to students of mid-nineteenth-century culture, what-ever their disciplinary allegiance, and interrogated them, seeking to identify across and between them discourses that manifest the complexity of Pre-Raphaelitism as a project and the diverse and contradictory character of its well-known appeals to personality, to fantasy, to a medieval past, to an ideal of femininity, and so on. We thus reclaim the ground of pictorial imagery for the historical enquiry that incorporates also questions of visual and verbal rhetoric. Thus, for example, whilst the material history of Holman Hunt's Middle East paintings (rooted in questions of patronage and the market) is not ignored in this book, that history is opened up as part of a broader colonialist history (at once psychic and public) that can only be fully understood by mapping the similarities and differences between languages in circulation, whether visual or verbal.

1

Brothers in their anecdotage: Holman Hunt's Pre-Raphaelitism and the Pre-Raphaelite Brotherhood
Laura Marcus

In so far as the Movement was – as in the days of the P.R.B. – a secret or closed society; or a group of more widely spread individuals – as in its later phases – possessing an esoteric sense of elitism, the thoughts and actions of its members, to themselves or to each other, were matters of the liveliest interest. This feeling of belonging to an artistic aristocracy, such as the Bloomsbury Group possessed, is one which fosters the literature of letter, diary and memoir writing: and it is a literature of which the Pre-Raphaelites in their posterity might well be proud. (Stanford, p. 16)

This now familiar construction of the artist as solitary genius transcending the conventions of his age was circulated and popularized in the latter decades of the century through the expanding literature of artistic biography. . . . It was through this genre that the controversy unleashed by the claims made in the 1880's on behalf of Rossetti's pre-eminence was fought out. But it is this literature of partisan apologia and self-justification which is now mistreated by modern art historians as if it were merely an historical archive. (Cherry and Pollock, *Art history*, Dec. 1984, p. 484)

The history of Pre-Raphaelitism is such that any discussion of the movement will, at some juncture, need to address the question of the personal writings produced by and about the Pre-Raphaelites. A fairly banal reason for this exists: the difficulty of ignoring material – letters, diaries, memoirs and biographies – in such volume. Of course, the very fact that this material was and has continued to be deemed worthy of preservation and publication attests to a more complex issue: given that such literature in large part defines the meanings of 'Pre-Raphaelitism', it is not immediately apparently what form the concept of the movement would take if it were not brought into consideration.

The question I wish to raise here is that of the ways in which the memoir-form should be approached. In the quotations above, two polarised views are represented: the first celebrates the richness and diversity of expressions of the individual in relation to the privileged group – an 'artistic aristocracy' – while the second offers a twofold critique of the biographical form and the uses to which it is put. The genre, Deborah Cherry and Griselda Pollock assert, contributes to an art history negatively defined as near wholly concerned with the history of artists – thus functioning as an obstacle to the development of more historically, politically and culturally informed analyses. Furthermore, memoirs, biographies and autobiographies come to function as history for the art historian, despite the very specific conditions of their production and circulation; a resource for anecdote and interpretation which both consolidates the overweening concern with individual lives and becomes a substitute for those archival materials which could become the basis for a materialist art history.

These two alternatives – the celebration of memoir-writing or a total rejection of the biographical form – do not, of course, exhaust the possibilities of reading and critically employing personal writings. But the location of workable approaches is not a simple task. The relationship between history, art and biography has a long and complex history of its own. It is worth noting, in the light of Cherry and Pollock's discussion, that Thomas Carlyle was writing in 1832: 'Even in the highest works of Art, our interest, as the critics complain, is too apt to be strongly or even mainly of a biographic sort. In the Art we can nowise forget the Artist . . .' (Carlyle, p. 52). Carlyle defends the biographical on the grounds that 'History is the essence of innumerable biographies'; neither art nor history exist without Man. In the late twentieth century we are no doubt still living with the nineteenth-century legacy of this 'biographical age of ours', as Carlyle called it. But it is not a legacy that has gone unquestioned. In the field of literature, the history of twentieth-century literary criticism can be charted almost wholly in relation to its negotiations with and circumventions of biographical materials, in the attempt to shift biography from its privileged position as evidence for and explication of literary meanings. One such theoretical strategy, particularly relevant to the present discussion, has been the focus on biography and autobiography as autonomous *literary* genres: the memoir-form, when turned into an object of literary study in its own right, can no longer convincingly operate as authenticating evidence for the production and meanings of fictional works. If the 'life' is turned into 'text', lives and letters become homologous structures.

Such a strategy, of course, creates problems of its own. The emphasis on the 'textuality' of lives may invove a rejection of the concept of a sovereign author expressing his essential self through the literary work, but it also serves to reconfirm, in troubling ways, the status of the fictional and literary as a universal discourse. Troubling, because literature was in part granted such status precisely because it was seen to understand and express more profoundly than any other form of knowledge or belief the essence of what constituted Man. We have, it seems, moved from one idealist position to another, and the biographical, though emerging in a representational rather than referential guise, remains intact.

It is clearly no less tenacious within art history, although the forms it takes and the uses to which it is put are not identical to those within literature. The very fact that within art history writing serves to endorse visual meanings rather than other forms of writing creates a different set of hierarchies; it is also the case that written accounts tend to be employed less analytically and more evidentially in art historical practice than in contemporary literary theory. Although I have been critical of the idealism implicit in the 'textualising' of lives, I would also claim that such approaches have often usefully questioned the traditional functions of the memoir-form as either documentary evidence or pure individual self-expression. They have also required a closer analysis of the different forms such writings take (which I have so far tended to homogenise), questioning, for example, the received wisdom that letters and journals are temporally, and by extension essentially, closer to the 'truth' of self or event than more fully narrativised and retrospective forms such as memoirs and autobiographies. The further step to be taken, however, involves an interrogation of the relationship between biography, history and cultural production in ways which do not merely privilege the literary mode and which move us beyond the biographical impasse.

At this point, however, we need briefly to consider what is meant by biography and what is seen to distinguish it, as in Cherry and Pollock's account, from history. In the nineteenth century, the tradition of fact-gathering and research for the purposes of biography was institutionalised, in opposition to an earlier tradition of impressionistic memoir, and the life was seen to be validated by documentary evidence. We are thus confronted with the parodox that the 'romance' of the individual life was seen as inseparable from a belief in historical fact. The version of history apparent here is a positivist one, in which events are referred back to experience as the basis of truth. If we critique the biographical mode, then, for its undue emphasis on individual experience, we must also implicate certain forms of historical understanding, rather than positing an entity called 'history' which exists in opposition to 'biography', and acts as a corrective to its flaws and limitations. As a related point, it would seem that it is not wholly adequate to posit a fundamental distinction between the 'primary', unmediated forms of history offered by the archive, and the partisan forms of narrative history and biography. A materialist history by definition involves a commitment to concrete historical research, but it does not logically follow that the return to the archive will of necessity produce a materialist history. Its materials, as the nineteenth-century example reveals, can always be employed to give credence and substance to the individual life and individual experience.

It is possible, then, to reach towards an understanding of conceptions of history through an examination, as opposed to an eschewal, of the biographical mode. Moving from the question of history to that of individualism, my arguments so far have suggested that an emphasis on the individual life and individual experience is always misplaced. This is clearly not perceived to be the case in recent working-class and women's history, where the biographical and autobiographical form becomes a central aspect of the articulation of lives outside dominant cultural narratives, and is seen to differ significantly from its 'bourgeois individualist' counterparts. It would seem, therefore, that the issue is not only that of what history but of whose. I would question, without in any way criticising the political motivations behind such a position, an absolute distinction between valid and invalid forms of self-expression, in part because self-expression is not the sole issue. More relevant is the question of self-conceptions, and it is these that can be approached through the biographical mode. If we reject personal writings on the grounds of their rampant individualism, or, in the case of the artist's biography and autobiography, their role in perpetuating myths about artists, we exclude from discussion a major body of material which has contributed not only to definitions of Pre-Raphaelitism but, more broadly, to cultural conceptions of the artist as subject. The remainder of this chapter will focus on Pre-Raphaelite memoir-writing, and in particular Holman Hunt's autobiographical text, as a way of critically exploring self-conceptions, using them analytically as materials towards a recasting of the concept of the author/artist, and examining how the relationships between art, history, and the individual life are represented in autobiographical texts.

Holman Hunt's *Pre-Raphaelitism and the Pre-Raphaelite Brotherhood* was first published in two volumes in 1905, when the author was seventy-eight, and in a revised edition in 1913, three years after his death. The early edition is 1,000 pages long, and charts the progress of Hunt's life in chronological fashion, with clearly demarcated distinctions between 'life-stages', childhood, youth, maturity and age. In the childhood, Hunt presents the development of self as artist, from his infantile passion for drawing onwards. Youth is constituted in large part by the account of his friendship with Millais and the formation of the Brotherhood. In this section Hunt dramatises their debates over the nature and functions of art against the background of departures, and returns from town to country, from studio to Nature as studio. In a representation of the Brothers as troubadours, the world becomes their stage. Hunt's travels to the Orient constitute 'maturity'; isolated and beleaguered by hostile 'natives' (and hostile reviewers back in England), Hunt represents himself as engaged in solitary battles for the honour of art and the nation, and in seeking the past in a degraded present for the sake of the future. The return to England consolidates maturity, and here Hunt represents himself in dialogue with the great national and artistic figures of the Victorian age – Ruskin, Tennyson and Palgrave. In this dialogue with the voices that speak the best of Englishness, Hunt consolidates an image of national identity, before moving in the Retrospect of the autobiography to become the prophetic voice in the fullness of age. The artist's life is thus represented as a mission, life-stages being the stages along the journey which ends not with mortality but with the single voice that speaks to posterity of the transcendence of time.

The *Times literary supplement* reviews of the 1905 and 1913 editions of Hunt's text reveal a little about its critical reception. The earlier review is laudatory, claiming that Hunt, as the member most steadfastly dedicated to the Pre-Raphaelite 'faith', is 'the man of all others best fitted to tell the story of their prime', and that the memoir 'has a three-fold interest – historical, artistic and human' (3 Dec. 1905, pp. 425–6). History, art and life are thus seen to exist in happy conjuncture within the autobiographical text. The later review is near wholly critical, and the reviewer takes particular exception to the title of Hunt's work:

. . . the two volumes are not so much a history of a movement or a Brotherhood as the autobiography of Holman Hunt himself. . . . It is regrettable that a book which might have had permanent value as the record of an interesting movement in the history of British art should contain so many pages about personal squabbles which have no historical or artistic importance. (16 April 1914, p. 183).

In this account, autobiography has been employed at the expense of history and art, and individualism is perceived to be at odds with an historical or collective representation. In contrast to the earlier review, the life is seen to fail to ramify beyond its individual context or to contain history within itself.

Although William Michael Rossetti is not mentioned in the review, it is apparent from other sources that he came to be viewed as the most reliable of the Pre-Raphaelite 'historians', perhaps because he was the most apparently self-effacing. I would argue that Hunt's memoir functions as the antithesis of Rossetti's muted tomes, and that whereas William Fredeman describes Hunt's text as 'the most prejudiced of the memoirs' (Fredeman, 1965, p. 27), it was precisely part of Hunt's strategy to claim authority over definitions and histories by repudiating the role of conscientious recorder. This becomes most apparent in the early sections of Hunt's memoir, in which dialogues, particularly between himself and Millais, run for some twenty pages. It is not credibility with which Hunt is concerned here: his apparent fascination with the Millais family clearly operates in part as a denial of this role to its more usual incumbents, the Rossettis, and the excesses of speech and rhetoric are intended to construct a dialogue across history within which Dante Gabriel is for the most part silenced.

By contrast, W. M. Rossetti's *Some reminiscences*, a two-volume autobiography published a year after Hunt's, draws particular attention to the problem of dialogue in autobiography:

> For some matters I have a moderately fair memory – I might mention dates in particular. But there are two kinds of things for which my memory is decidedly bad – the faces of people I meet, and the words of conversations. When a conversation is over, I am not long in forgetting even its definite purport, and more especially I recollect scarcely at all the precise words that had been used. Naturally therefore, when I come to write reminiscences, I can say little of the talks which I had, even with men of mark, and I could very seldom give a resume of their actual phrases. To invent diction which would convey the same sense in a certain way is what I do not feel at liberty to do. The result is that these pages of mine are most rarely enlivened with a few words of remembered talk: which is a pity, but under the circumstances it cannot be helped. (W. M. Rossetti, 1906, xi).

Implicit in Rossetti's statement is an argument about the relationship between fiction and history, and his denial of fabrication as a possible strategy in autobiography links back to the nineteenth-century emphasis on the role of fact and documentary within personal writings to which I referred earlier. But it is not adequate to set Hunt against Rossetti as an opposition between fabrication and documentation. It is rather Hunt's belief in the power of the voice which functions in marked distinction to W. M. Rossetti's faithful transcriptions of the written materials of diary, memoir and journal and his self-appointed role as scribe and recorder. Hunt opens the Preface to his memoir with an epigram from Theocritus: 'I am but a single voice' (1, p. vii). This quotation focuses three central issues: the speaking voice (as opposed to the writing subject), uniqueness and self-identity, and the image of the lone voice crying in the wilderness, the voice of the prophet-seer. All three are combined in the Preface and Retrospect to the memoir, and it is this autobiographical 'frame' that demonstrates most clearly Hunt's strategies.

Hunt opens and closes the text with pronouncements on the past, present and future states of art. Human life, we are told in the Preface, is not long enough for the attainment of maturity in art, but the Greeks, Romans and Italians, by the handing on of wisdom, 'extended individual life'. From the present from which Hunt speaks, the dying-out of the apprenticeship system means this is no longer possible. This situation can only be ameliorated if the artist adopts the traditions of his nation, aligning himself with the Great Tradition of Chaucer, Shakespeare and Milton, while simultaneously allowing Nature to become his mentor and tutor: '. . . how will a people be blessed as were those to whom the artist gave a national talisman for the conquest of ignorance and brutality. Art, as of old, should stamp a nation's individuality, it should be the witness of its life to all eternity.' If these lessons are not heeded, vigour will decay and 'the everlasting dignity of the natural proportions of the human form' will become deformed, (1, p. xiii). This is elaborated further in the conclusion of the text: 'The present feeling towards art . . . is altogether dead to any thought of its never-ending universal preciousness' (2, p. 452). Here Hunt's attack is directed towards contemporary artists ignorant of the nature of the materials they use. The old masters 'despised no drudgery that would contribute to the permanence of their work', while the modern painter 'knows not that certain pigments put into conjunction will vitiate each other's permanence' (2, p. 453). Many paintings of Reynolds, Wilkie and Hilton, amongst others, are 'doomed to complete destruction' through their use of asphaltum as a ground: 'in the early century time had not yet revealed the disastrous consequences of using the pernicious Dead Sea pitch' (2, p. 454) while bitumen, 'a preparation from Egyptian corpses' (2, p. 455), has ruined Landseer's early pictures and there are still painters using it as a result of their indifference to the permanence of their work. From this discussion of materials we move directly to the question of art and the nation: 'National obligations require that to compete in excellence with other nations we must never abandon cultural principles, for our art, like any other, has certain inevitable conventions, and if all arts are put aside, certain it is that the stability of the nation is doomed, and sottish barbarism will reign supreme' (2, p. 459).

In the Retrospect, France, and its espousal of Impressionism, became object lessons; painters and their subjects indulge in orgies and the nation is in a state of decadence and decline. 'The purpose of art', the closing lines of the memoir assert, 'is, in love of guileless beauty, to lead man to distinguish between that which, being clean in spirit, is productive of virtue and that which is flaunting and meretricious and productive of ruin to a Nation' (2, p. 493). In these passages, Hunt's role becomes that of sage and prophet: the bearer and dispenser, to borrow Terry Eagleton's account of the Victorian critic, of 'a generalized ideological wisdom . . . one whose synoptic vision, undimmed by any narrowly technical interest, is able to survey the whole cultural and intellectual landscape of his age' (Eagleton, 1984, p. 45). But Hunt's is a belated and near-obsolete contribution to this Victorian context; moreover, as artist rather than 'man of letters', he must turn 'technical interest' into 'synoptic vision' through maverick analogising, in which the stability of paint becomes tantamount to the stability of nations. (The use of deadly Eastern substances like bitumen spells decay and degradation.) It is in part, however, through such rhetorical devices that he can lay claim to a synoptic vision: association and analogy provide him with the authority to speak for history, charting, like Gibbon, the decline of empires, or, like Carlyle, a panoply of heroes.

Such passages also reveal Hunt's negotiations with the problems involved in writing autobiography, which are not distinct from the prophetic 'vocalisations' of his Preface and Retrospect, but are fully implicated in questions of time, history and identity. In order to explore these questions further, I want to turn to an autobiographical precedent for Hunt, Benvenuto Cellini's *Autobiography* (begun in 1558), and to suggest that the tradition of artistic autobiography is a sub-genre within which Hunt's work can be contextualised. Like Hunt, Cellini capitalises on the 'talking' aspect of his text, insisting that the major part of the work is dictated, and thus by implication that it is both unrhetorical and unmediated. This emphasis has fuelled critical beliefs that Cellini is characteristic of his age, and that his autobiography is a direct transcription of life. Cellini comes to represent – and represents himself – as the ideal Renaissance man: an iconic figure who is both artist and soldier, and for whom the aesthetic and action are not separate spheres of existence. He thus resides over the realm of deed, action and teleology, but also creates art capable of transcending the moment. The present of the text is both a durational moment and partakes of the extra-durational time of the world of art. Cellini thus resides over both sets of time, and in his concern with classical time, both conserves and extends the past into the present. Such a maintenance of identity in time can be viewed, I suggest, as one of the classical problems of autobiography, and Cellini in part resolves it through the illusion of voice and immediate presence. We find here the belief that dialogue – speech *en face* – makes speakers both ontologically and temporally present to each other: the voice generates meanings and writing is simply a device to record the voice. Cellini, in dramatising this belief, comes to preside over the meaning of his voice, and in the identity of time and value is seen (and sees himself) as the best symbol of his age.

The deployment of significantly similar structures in Hunt's text clarifies a number of his rhetorical strategies. It puts into question the nomination of the nineteenth-century novel (see Cherry and Pollock's account) as the model for Hunt's autobiographical form: in generic terms, Hunt's text is, like Cellini's, certainly closer to the 'picaresque' mode, each stage of his journey being marked by an adventure and the creation of a work of art. Through the links with Cellini it is also possible to point to particular structures of the self-conceptions and cultural conceptions of the artist which retain a certain constancy. Hunt's representation of himself as artist–soldier on his journeys to the East, 'with a large sketch book on my back, and a gun on my saddle' (2, p. 70), is discussed by Marcia Pointon in Chapter 2 of this book. I want to point to the frequency with which Hunt makes the comparison between the soldier's and the artist's contributions to the nation: the difference for Hunt lies less in the nature of their activities than in the country's failure to appreciate the artist–militant's endeavours. 'I also had been trying to do the State some service but alone' (2, p. 83; the reference to Othello's final speech, 'I have done the State some service and they know't', is obscure). I would argue that Hunt seeks for his self-presentation the iconic image of Renaissance man, and a similar governance over the durational and non-durational modes of time. This is revealed as anxiety when it comes to the question of his role as historian of the Movement, which demands that he place its members in time while simultaneously arguing against the ephemerality of Pre-Raphaelitism as artistic project and vision. In other words, a biographer such as W. M. Rossetti would, in Hunt's terms, be failing the spirit of the Movement by claiming for it history but not immortality.

The desired relationship to time and identity is reinforced by Hunt's representation of the Biblical world, his equivalent to Cellini's Classical Greece. 'Fidelity to nature' becomes a complex issue here, for Hunt seeks an ideal past in the present of the 'degraded society' through which he travels. (Marcia Pointon explores this relationship as manifested in his paintings.) Racial theory, and particularly the theory of the 'degradation of types' is not a theme I intend to examine here, other than to point to the ways in which it complicates the Pre-Raphaelites' appeal to 'fidelity to nature'. For whereas Hunt at times celebrates his discovery of 'interesting examples of the ancient national type' (2, p. 382) or a 'kaleidoscope of noble pictures of early humanity about me' (2, p. 389), he also disclaims the purely documentary nature of his role as artist–ethnographer:

It must not be supposed that an artist in honestly using his model does not obey the principle of selection. He has to eschew all marks of degradation or unsuitability in the person before him which would not be consistent with the character that he has in mind, exercising the same fastidious choice as in the theme he treats. . . . (2, p. 32)

Questions of racial identity and the suitability of artistic subjects thus become inextricably linked: '. . . the habit of Orientals to sit cross-legged from infancy tends to destroy the delicate form of the man's lower limbs; from this cause I had some difficulty in satisfying myself in the painting of the figure, which occasioned many undoings of my work. . . .' (2, p. 292)

It has been noted elsewhere that Hunt's text is shot through with British imperialist ideology: '. . . the artist performs the particularized function of providing a means of vicarious possession by an authenticated representation (I was there and saw what I faithfully record)' (Cherry and Pollock, Art history, Dec. 1984, p. 486). I would add, however, that Hunt's project entails an erasure of history in its search for a concept of the past, and that it is this writing out of a people's time that marks the imperialist enterprise as much as the attempt to possess the present.

The function of the written text as 'supplementary' to visual representation is thus in part to mark the difference between an ideal past and origin and the 'degraded society' of the present, the latter being unsuitable for art, though not for writing. It is the image of 'degradation' and the need to control or reverse it that runs throughout the text as an anxiety. I have pointed to the ways in which Hunt asserts command over time, both in his relationship to the Orient as artist and traveller, and as autobiographer, speaking from outside time, and in a 'single voice', of the past made present for posterity. Arresting the flux of time, fixing the meanings of artistic representation through typology, demonstrating the corrosive effects of substances upon paintings and immorality upon the nation – Hunt's autobiographical and artistic strategies are mobilised to guard against damage to the image, to self-image and to history.

I have suggested that Hunt's text needs to be read in the context of nineteenth- and early twentieth-century debates about the 'proper' modes of representing lives – the view that biography has a national, institutional function in transmitting the achievements of one generation to the next. I have further stated that Hunt demonstrates the particular need of the *auto*-biographer to maintain identity in time, and that his concern with the fixity and stability of images operates as analogue for the ways in which 'life' and 'art' function together. Memoir-writings, then, can offer an insight into the historical, the artistic and the individual as *conceptions* which have particular relevance to contemporary discuss-ions about the relationship of the biographical to cultural production.

It is also questionable, returning to my opening discussion, whether a materialist art history would be achieved through the mere refusal to engage with the biographical dimension of art history. As my earlier example from literary studies suggests, the biographical, if merely repressed, has an uncanny way of returning in other guises. A more effective approach is to engage with the biographical directly, and to critically interrogate biography, autobiography and the 'lives and letters' form. If we examine the nature of the relationship between history, biography and art more closely, we may loosen the bond between the history of art and lives of artists.

2

The artist as ethnographer:
Holman Hunt and the Holy Land
Marcia Pointon

Holman Hunt's journeys to the Middle East, forming as they do a major portion of his autobiography, have not been overlooked by art historians. However, whilst the problematic nature of Hunt's relationship to the Orient has been recognised, it has been explained in terms of a romantic fascination, 'a love affair with the Middle East', and as an experience that gave the artist access to a world of light and colour that affected his manner of painting (Landow, 1982, pp. 648, 653).

In this chapter I shall be offering an account of Hunt's travels which challenges an opposition between a 'love affair' and 'hardship and difficulties' and questions what, if anything, it might mean – other than the choice of new colours on the palette – to 'see with new eyes' (Landow, 1982). I shall look at the construction of a form of biblical painting in the framework of colonial power. I shall examine how and why the European artist–traveller orders the spaces of the Oriental other and, finally, identifies the represented body of Christ as the object of narcissistic desire, the space that is to be occupied by the colonialist authority. Essential to colonial discourse is the travel narrative, an account of arrivals and departures. This, too, is my starting point.

In November 1854, Hunt, aged twenty-seven, was in the Middle East, sketching and making preliminary studies for a number of paintings. He had begun his journey in January and spent some time in Cairo and Giza with his fellow-artist Thomas Seddon. The two men travelled down the Nile to Damietta and via Jaffa to Palestine. Hunt made trips to Wadi Kerith, Hebron and the Dead Sea in the summer months. The late autumn found him wishing to spend an extended period at the Dead Sea in order to paint *The Scapegoat*.[1] Hunt was an educated and well-prepared traveller. In Cairo he reported himself to be re-reading Herodotus, Sir Gardner Wilkinson, the Bible and Lane's *Modern Egyptians* (Hunt, 1905, 1, 377).[2] Although the prime object of his journey was the accumulation of visual evidence, he wrote many letters and also kept a diary on which he drew when preparing his two-volume memoirs nearly half a century later. Hunt's diaries survive in manuscript and further evince his familiarity with the conventions of nineteenth-century travel writing.[3]

A comparison between the manuscript version of a particular event and the representation of that event published many years later by an elderly artist who had acquired authority and status is not to suggest that the first is unvarnished truth and the second a fabrication. The first is already an edited response, organised in the act of writing. A comparison is a means of registering difference: difference between the private record and the public announcement, between the young man's voice as speaking subject and the old man's pronouncement, between 1854 and the 1880s when Hunt first began to publish his account.[4] Here is Hunt in his manuscript diary, recording on 15 November his efforts to obtain from the local Arab population the necessary support for his expedition to the Dead Sea. The sustained narrative and the control of language can be seen here to be commensurate with the contradictory colonial rule of father and oppressor (Bhabha, p. 74):

Notwithstanding the strongest efforts to control my humour while making necessary complaints and exhortations I was sorry to find myself possessed of so much anger as I rode along in front on my slow beast that even the beautiful [hills] sunshine could not dissipate for some time. . . . I was asked to dismount as the Sheik come ove[r] to salute me. he is a tall savage with a [dark] dusky long face which struck me to resemble a mules – he walked in a slow prowling manner – and when I [stept] moved forward one step he grasped my hand and held it sedately – grinning in my face as he does to his subjects before they [place] bow their heads together in embracing, as it occurred to me that he was waiting for this last profession of friendship I stared at him in English fashion and nodded turning to give orders about my tent – men in twenties flocked out and placed themselves around me looking at my gun, and mimicking my bad arabic one to another while the children were evidently on the look out for anything that might fall in their way. In this position I told the Sheik I would talk to him after a little while and made my way to a [stone] rock at a stone's throw, on which I sat alone for ten minutes until the tent was fixed – my entrance to the tent was a signal for the Sheik who came, and sat down opposite to me – holding out his empty pipe for tobacco. I made Nicola (Hunt's servant) fill this, and mine and then I divided a quantity at hand between him and Saleh – my old guide. I then informed him that I wanted to go to the Wady Zuara for 15 days adding that I had a letter from the English Consul which I delivered to him, he cannot read but he solemnly received it, folded it three times and put it into his pouch when seeing it to be a good opportunity as there were thirty or forty men looking on I took out the coat and put it upon his shoulders adding 'this is a backsheesh from the English Consul for you.' I think [it] I performed my part with a sedateness and an air of importance which would have won [lasting] repeated bursts of laughter from *my poor dead friend*

Walter Deverell. Abou was not to be outdone however for he stood up gravely and had it adjusted by my servant, and then reseated himself without a smile until he had finished his pipe and coffee. When he rose and walked away promising to return an hour after sunset.

The next day Hunt resumed his journal after watching Arab children tormenting two fowls. The topos of Arab stupidity is now shifted into the topos of Oriental cruelty:

> I thought the whole race of arabs were a blot on the face of the earth . . . as he walked away in his find [sic] red cloth coat, which I had bought him, huddled over a dirty gibeah and under a coarse abbiah, which with his dusky, dirty thick skin made him look about as much grander as a fine coat beautifies a monkey – or mongrel dog. (MS Ryl.)

The stylistic amendments that are in evidence in the corrections to the manuscript are carried a great deal further in the version of this account published with the authority of the full-length book on Pre-Raphaelitism in 1905. Most significant, however, is the subtle shift in power relations that is established by changing the terrain. Now Hunt sends for the Sheik who has to walk up a hill and there is no suggestion of the artist being obliged to dismount. Moreover, a note of optimism is introduced, with the substitution of an experience of enjoyment of the natural beauties of the countryside for the passage of anger which is the prelude to the encounter with the Sheik – the litigious, lying native that was a central object of nineteenth-century colonial regulation (Bhabha, p. 79) – and by the interpellation of classical and biblical texts between Hunt as subject and the object of his mission. The opening description of the published version thus offers us an uninhabited, natural terrain, a free space into which the raconteur can inscribe his claims to ownership. It is a terrain already familiar in travel literature from the eighteenth century onwards:

> The wilderness of Ziph was seen from every fresh hill brow, nowhere was there a trace of landmark, road, or any sign of the rule which gregarious man ordains for common interest or protection . . . the bare earth grew wilder as though new from the Creator's hand; and yet I felt a novel joy in life. I looked around to account for my exhilaration of spirit, and could only discover a sweet purity in the very barrenness of the scene before me; . . . Separation of this kind leads man to the understanding of the poet shepherd's aspiration when he sang, 'my soul thirsteth after thee, my flesh longeth for thee: in a barren and dry land where no water is.'

> In the afternoon I arrived at the encampment of Abou Daouk, the sheik of whom I was in search. When my tent was pitched, I sent word that I was expecting a visit from him, and as he came up the slope I stepped out to welcome him. He had a long face with large projecting teeth and a long but retiring chin, and as he

neared me, looking his affablest, I could not help thinking how like a mule he was. I had to adopt an English tone of preoccupation with Nicola, to make sure that he should not expect me to fall on his dirty person and in Arab fashion embrace him. When he was seated on a raised mat at my door, I delivered greetings from the Consul, and made Nicola unwrap the parcel containing a *jabbah* of brightest scarlet, which I then placed on his shoulders. The contrast of the vivid colour with his grimy visage made him look dustier than ever, and I wondered whether the good Omar appeared so polluting, when the Patriarch, giving up to him the keys of Jerusalem, muttered, 'Surely this is the abomination which maketh desolate'. (Hunt, 1905, 1, 466–7)

Hunt's accounts comprise a combination of narrative and descriptive discourse of a genre which, it has been established, has been a feature that modern ethnography inherited from earlier travel writing (Pratt, p. 38). His text is a mixture of generalisations, eye-witness anecdotes, and personal irony. The frustration and depression of the primary text, typical of what has been called 'the gruff Victorian explorer–adventurer' is transformed in the secondary text into the account of a benevolent and all-powerful traveller attaining his goal with no difficulty. Like the ethnographer, Hunt's credibility has to rest ultimately on the power of his description; as an artist he also has to extend the data of the verbal record, as well as its rhetoric, into a visual equivalent. Just how this happens will be examined in due course. Whilst the public initially received only the visual record, this was subsequently endorsed by the verbal account published in full in 1905 to which all cataloguers and historians invariably refer. Words thus legitimise image. Hunt's commitment to 'truth' and his desire to record things fast disappearing place him in close affinity with the early ethnographic recorders. His companion during the first part of his 1854 visit, Thomas Seddon, concentrated on views; for Hunt the object of his enquiry was manners and customs.

Hunt's 1854 journey to the Middle East was later constructed by him as a gradual descent into the primitive, commencing with the voyage from Marseilles to Malta in the company of Indian officials and ladies returning from leave. During the course of the voyage he ponders on the greatness of the British Empire. He recounts to Thomas Combe how a boy of only seven but 'a perfect little Englishman in respect to a sense of superiority' assaulted an 'Islamite' of sixteen or seventeen who had offended him 'with perfect success and did not desist until he had obtained enough submission for attention to his caution that he always might expect such punishment for such rudeness to Englishmen . . .' (MS Coombe, 1 Feb. 1854). This contrasts with the anarchy and disintegration of class order on board the Nile steamer ('it was obvious that the costumes and pretensions . . . could not be taken as their true social credentials'). Finally, in Cairo, 'business went on in primaeval fashion as it might have done in the days of Jacob' (Hunt, 1905, 1, pp. 369, 372, 373). 'The unshipment of the cargo was performed by a hundred or more natives who all groaned under their loads like camels as they moved me to wrath by their stupid leisureliness . . .' (MS Coombe, 1 Feb. 1854). Hunt saw manners and customs passing away and felt his obligation to be, like that of the ethnographer, the process of recording for posterity.

The most intense moments are recorded in the present tense, a strategy that is clearly intended to lend veracity and is employed in the journals themselves. A passage in the 1855 diary, which was not transcribed in *Pre-Raphaelitism and the Pre-Raphaelite brotherhood*, describes the miracle of the Holy Fire at the Church of the Sepulchre, which Hunt found deeply disturbing, and does so mainly in the present tense: 'a party of about 50 men and boys are tearing round and round screaming, clapping hands, stamping, and all to an unearthly wild chanting continuous shout. None dressed but in white unbleached linen shirt – all with legs naked. Some all their bodies uncovered . . .' (MS Ryl., 7 April 1855).

The ethnographer, it has been pointed out, works as a sort of translator, yet no primary text that can be read by others survives his own. He or she decodes the message and interprets. The message must be made convincing – it treats of the strange, the foreign and the unbelievable, that which challenges belief. The truth of the message is everything. The present tense in Hunt's journals is a strategy for establishing this truth. But Hunt's enterprise differs from that of the ethnographers in so far as his ethnographic account is then the raw material for a *reconstruction* in another medium of what he believes to have happened at an earlier time.

Of Cairo Hunt later wrote: 'All the traditional manners were threatening to pass away, together with ancient costume and hereditary taste; I saw that in another generation it would be too late to reconstruct the past, save in rural and desert life, if even there (Hunt, 1905, 1, p. 377). Yet there was nothing populist in his project to paint *The Miracle of the Holy Fire*. Cairo did, indeed, change beyond all recognition, as Hunt discovered when revisiting the city in 1892. The event which he had witnessed in 1855 in the Church of the Sepulchre in such a frenzy of embarrassment ('I am disgusted yet must stay') is now represented in 1893 by Hunt in a spirit of scientific conservatism and the painting regarded as an esoteric object whose meaning is accessible only to the learned few (1):

> Whether the celebration is regarded with shame by the advocates of unflinching truth, or with toleration as suitable to the ignorance of the barbaric pilgrims for whom it is retained, or with adoration by those who believe the fire to be miraculous, it has been from early centuries regarded as of singular importance . . . and every year the survival of the early record must be more valued. I exhibited this picture at the New Gallery, and afterwards lent it to Liverpool; I then determined to retain it in my own house as being of a subject understood in its importance only by the few. (Hunt, 1905, 2, pp. 385–6)

If travel literature and ethnography provided Hunt with one set of discourses, it is within controversies over art and religious truth that Hunt's enterprise must also be located. Laying claim to the Other in its sense both of another place and another time was, for Hunt, merely a part of engaging with the theological and social problem of a contemporary Christianity. Colonial trophies could be intellectual and imaginative as well as material. And for Hunt – at least potentially – they were both. Archaeological and biblical knowledge allied with the power of the brush would permit Hunt to annexe the Middle East for the causes of Protestantism; he also thought of the material benefits of colonisation. Writing to Combe from Jerusalem early in July 1854, he spoke of seeing 'the corn being reaped by men and women who might have been the labourers of Boaz' then moves on to declare:

> I believe when the absurd notion about the dangers of this climate is corrected that many English people will immigrate here, instead of going to bleak uninteresting places like Australia or America. When I turn farmer, I shall certainly bring my father, mother and sisters here, keep a flock of camels and grow artichokes and palm trees. (MS Combe)

In the early nineteenth century, as Warner has pointed out, travel and religion intersected at the point of biblical archaeology. Critical investigation of biblical sites was undertaken by the American scholar Edward Robinson in 1838. The Palestine Exploration Fund was founded in 1865 and published its *Survey of Western Palestine* between 1881 and 1884 (M. Warner, 1984, p. 32 passim). Nochlin, following Said, has drawn attention to the implications for visual representation of myths concerning the timelessness of the Orient (Nochlin, 1983, p. 122). Hunt's comments in Cairo were parallelled in frequent declarations by fellow artists (M. Warner, 1984, p. 32); the ambivalence of the Westerner is profoundly evident for the value of what was deemed timeless was marketable precisely because it was threatened. The irony that underlies all ethnography, the fact that the very act of entering the domain where ancient

overleaf **1** W. Holman Hunt, *The miracle of the Holy Fire*

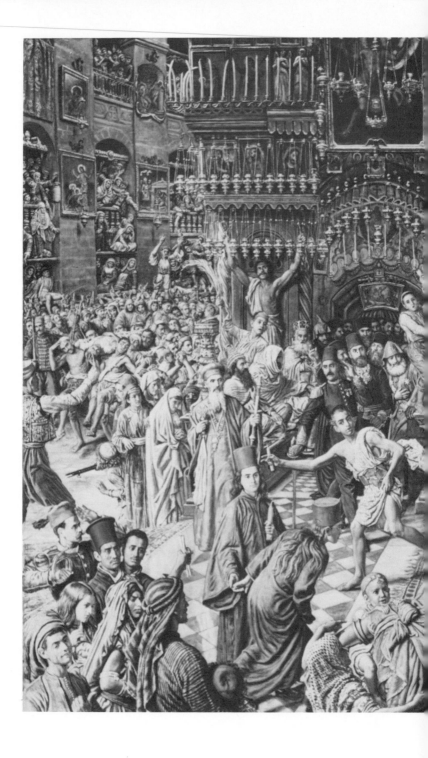

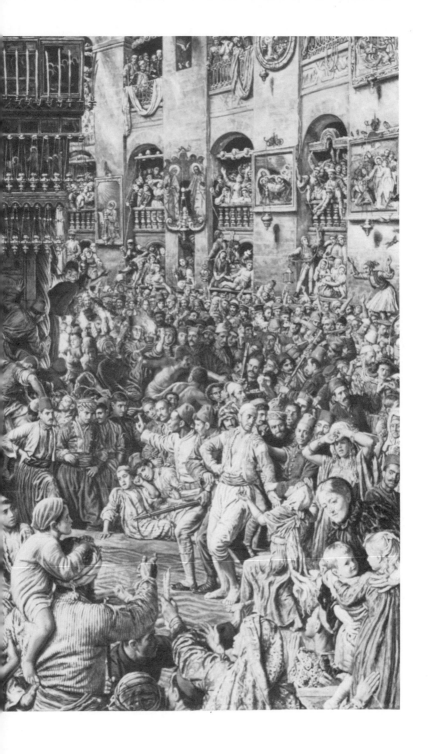

customs are thought to be maintained threatens the survival of those customs, also underlay the activities of traveller–artists.

Hunt's exasperation with the Arabs he encountered is to be located in the contradiction between a conviction that access to biblical truth lay in knowledge of the surviving manners of the Holy Land and a profoundly racist loathing of contemporary Arab life. Artists managed as long as they could treat living models as though they were landscapes or, like the Sphinx, immobile and motionless objects, lifeless models for the Western gaze. It was market conditions in the West that initiated the search for biblical–artistic truth; Horace Vernet, an astute French academic traveller–artist well aware of the popularity of Oriental subjects in France since Napoleon's Eastern campaigns, saw the way to uniting the Orientalist genre with the need for a revived form of Religious High Art. Vernet even employs a metaphor with powerful resonances of colonial mineral exploitation: 'Once the connection between Arab manners and customs and those of the ancient Hebrews takes hold of your thoughts . . . then the richest vein is yours to be mined!' (quoted M. Warner, 1984, p. 32). Wilkie, who visited the Holy Land in 1841, saw how this idea could be translated into Protestant terms. Archaeology could be used to create a space within which British artists could break with the corrupt conventions of a Roman Catholic Renaissance tradition of religious art. But what undoubtedly started off for Hunt as a desire to paint an authentic religious art with mass appeal rapidly became an arcane pursuit in which the learning that was a necessary adjunct to uncovering the past became an end in itself. Hunt kept *The miracle of the Holy Fire* (**1**) in his own possession, believing its importance would not be understood by the uninitiated, and felt that *The shadow of death* (**2**) was 'more fitted by itself for the Renan class of thinkers who have been studying the life of Christ as one particular branch of history' (*The Pre-Raphaelites*, no. 143). The conflict between popular appeal and learning remained an area of difficulty for Hunt; he complained bitterly to Archdeacon Farrar through the 1890s about lack of support for his work from the established Church and was resentful that he had been obliged to rely on brewers and tradesmen for the promulgation of his ideas (MSS Getty, 11 Feb. 1893 and through 1894).

As Landow and others have pointed out, artists of the period faced a host of problems resulting from the new concern with archaeological accuracy. The search for authenticity and for a new religious art relevant to the age was blurring the distinction between the secular and the religious that the Raphaelesque convention of the Grand Style had provided.

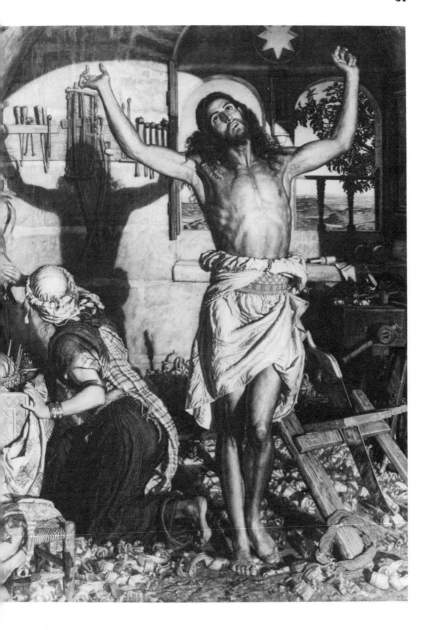

2 W. Holman Hunt, *The shadow of death*

Hunt's recollections suggest that preoccupation with religious emotion slid easily into preoccupation with emotion, that affect in the treatment of secular sensibility is not qualitatively different from the invocation of religious sentiment. To the end of his life, Hunt struggled with the difficult equation that proposed the religious function of a painting as separate from the artistic. While expressing disapproval of Pater and his Oxford followers (MS Getty, to Archdeacon Farrar, 7 Aug. 1894), he nonetheless dissociated himself from the view that 'because a purpose is a religious one the work of art must be good' (MS Getty, to Archdeacon Farrar, 5 June 1893). Attempts to address questions about Christ's appearance and, particularly, the introduction of detail derived from on-the-spot study in the Middle East, blurred the distinctions.

In 1847 Hunt was working on *Christ and the two Maries*, and experiencing difficulties. He recorded himself as having said at this time: 'I have been trying for some treatment that might make them see this Christ with something of the surprise that the Maries themselves felt on meeting Him as One who has come out of the grave, but I must for every reason put it by for the present.' He turns immediately to another subject, linking – as if by an inevitable bond – the spiritual and the sensual: 'In the meanwhile the story in Keats's *Eve of St. Agnes* illustrates the sacredness of honest responsible love and the weakness of proud intemperance, and I may practise my new principles to some degree on that subject'(**10**) (Hunt, 1905, 1, p. 85). Similarly, Rossetti's *the girlhood of Mary the Virgin* is presented as part of a triumvirate of women, the other two being famed for secular, if not sensual, rather than religious connotations: Margaret from *Faust* and Coleridge's Genevieve (Hunt, 1905, 1, p. 118). Hunt left *Christ and the two Maries* unfinished in 1847, returning to complete it nearly fifty years later. The relationship between aesthetic pleasure and spiritual pain and between pain in the material world and the expectation of spiritual pleasure beyond it were daunting. Struggling with the problem of representing the devotional love of the two Maries for Christ risen in flesh from the dead, it was an easy transition to the less problematic devotion of Porphyro to the body of Madeline.

The representation of the body of Christ presented particular problems in this era of authenticity. Hunt early rejected the notion that 'if doubtful about the treatment of our Lord' one should look 'at some of the Old Masters to be found in the Print Room' (Hunt, 1905, 1, p. 81). Study from the nude was, of course, the foundation of academic practice but biblical painting had invariably involved the draped figure and, in any case, study from the nude as productive of form did not help when it came to questions like skin tone or hair colouring for someone whose actual past life was being reconstructed. Hunt's declared view was that 'a man's work must be the reflex of a living image in his own mind, and not the icy double of the facts themselves' (Hunt, 1, p. 150). The interpellation of self, the foregrounding of subjectivity, was therefore crucial to the project of Protestant religious art. The modern mind made possible a painting which could 'express more fully and closely than had been possible in earlier days the nearness of God's appeal to Man through Revelation' (MS Getty, to Archdeacon Farrar, 11 Feb. 1893). Photography came to be regarded by 1870 as the best means of documentary illustration for contextualised biblical studies (MS Getty, to Archbishop Farrar, 1 July 1870); religious painting could thus fully embrace its distinctive destiny. The paintings that Hunt produced as a result of the Middle East journies differ markedly from the paintings he executed entirely at home. In particular they are characterised often by a dense and compact covering of fragmented surface detail which baffles the gaze in search of spatial coherence. In addition to the 1854–55 visit to the Holy Land, Hunt attempted to visit the Middle East in 1866 but got no further than Florence on account of a cholera epidemic. His second visit took place between 1869 and 1872, his third visit between 1875 and 1878 and his final visit in 1892. The paintings that are of particular interest are The lantern maker's courtship, The afterglow in Egypt, The finding of the Saviour in the temple(**3**) and The Scapegoat, all begun in Palestine during the first visit. The lantern maker . . . and The scapegoat were finished in 1856 back in England, The finding of the saviour . . . was finished in 1860 and The afterglow . . . in 1863. In addition Hunt brought back with him a great many landscape and figure studies, some of which were highly finished oils and watercolours. The shadow of death(**2**) and The triumph of the innocents were the chief results of the second visit, the first completed in 1873, the second worked on again during the third visit but not completed (due to a series of technical problems) until 1885. The miracle of the holy fire (**1**) was the product of the final visit although, as we have observed, the artist's verbal record dates back to 1855.[5] All these works were, of course, exhibited not in the Middle East but back in London where they were bought by the already mentioned 'tradesmen' and 'brewers', and, on occasion, by canny speculative dealers.

Immediately prior to his first journey to the Middle East, Hunt's main project was The light of the world (**4**). The problem of how to represent Christ was solved on this occasion by a means that differs markedly from the post-Middle East paintings. Hunt's main concern here was with the novelty of the idea; he engaged in lengthy researches (Maas) and was greatly alarmed when Elizabeth Siddall told him she had seen an old print of the same subject. The painting side-steps the issue of Christ's bodily presence by invoking the model of fairyland made popular by Fuseli, Dadd, Maclise and a succession of 'fairy painters' culminating in Joseph (later Sir Joseph) Noel Paton whose celebrated *Reconciliation of Oberon and Titania* was painted in 1847. Christ's clothing conceals and evades and is, therefore, divergent from the explicit sexual suggestiveness permitted to the painters of fairyland. But the setting is pure magic. Christ is an ungendered presence whose physicality is transposed into the tangible surroundings. His figure functions, therefore, in precisely the same relationship with its setting as the specifically gendered figures in *The awakening conscience* (**5**) do with theirs. Indeed, Hunt indicated that these two paintings formed something of a diptych (Landow, 1983, p. 473). Even allowing for some latitude in a painting that draws heavily on metaphor, the contrast between the bodyless Christ in *The light of the world* (**4**) and the tensile musculature and sweating body in *The shadow of death* (**2**) (a work that has been described as a commentory on *The light of the world*, Landow, 1972, p. 473) could hardly be more striking.

Hunt's message from the Holy Land had to be made convincing. If his verbal account established an effect of veracity by a variety of stylistic means, this also was true of the further transposition of that material into pictorial form. Like his 1905 book *Pre-Raphaelitism and the Pre-Raphaelite Brotherhood*, Hunt's paintings were composited productions, carefully organised to deliver the *effect* of authenticity. The most obvious way in which this could be achieved was, of course, by the introduction of a vast array of ethnographic detail such as typifies *The finding of the saviour in the temple* (**3**).[6] Ironically, the manufacture of this truth effect involved Hunt in a considerable deceit. In order to persuade Jewish men to sit for him in Jerusalem Hunt told them that his painting was no more than a depiction of a collection of rabbis (Hunt, 1905, 1, p. 422; *Contemporary review*, 1887, p. 213).

The effect of veracity is also dependent upon the myths of production that were intrinsic to the paintings from their very inception. Whilst Hunt did not publish his account until 1905, his travels were well known and the territory he had covered and, especially, the time the work had taken to complete, were well rehearsed in the press at exhibition time. In other words the build-up to exhibition was such as now attends the opening of a spectacular musical where the trailers are full of superlatives. 'After eighteen months spent at Jerusalem and nearly five years study, Mr. Hunt

3 W. Holman Hunt, *The finding of the Saviour in the temple*

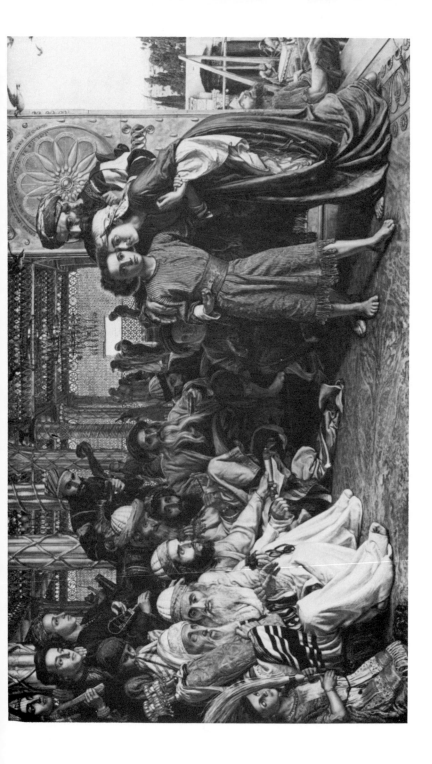

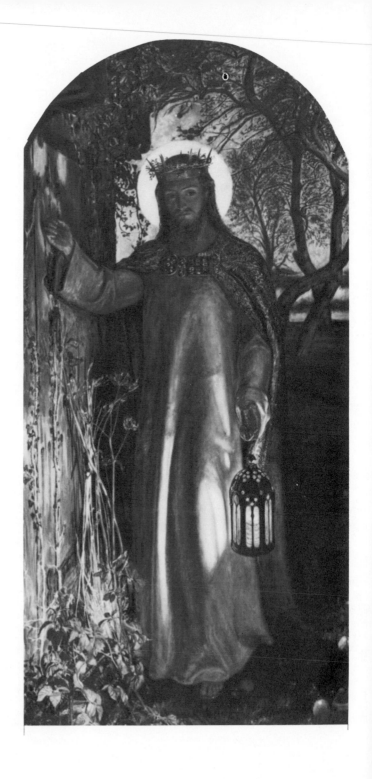

places his work before the public', reported the *Athenaeum*. Veracity is assured by the length of time devoted to the painting's production. Moreover, it is recognised that Hunt has well and truly appropriated his material; the Englishness of Hunt (unscathed and untainted by this long exposure to foreignness) and the national, Protestant, character of the painting are stressed in a way that is hard now to credit considering the plethora of specifically Jewish archaeological detail. The reception of this work thus evinces most clearly the particular proprietary nature of this Biblical–Colonialist representation:

... we are called upon to consider if it be worthy of the immense amount of time and labour employed upon it. No one will deny that the result is, in all respects, a grand one, and almost unequalled, in our time, for power of design and splendour of execution . . . Mr. Hunt is an essentially English painter, and has taken a thoroughly national idea of his work by representing Christ and the Virgin from a point of view which has seldom been attempted before . . . Thoroughly English and Protestant is the thought of showing the virgin as the mother and not as the spiritualised ideality of the early Italian painters, or in the sensuously beautiful type of those who succeeded them. (Bennett, 1969, no. 31)

Time was the element that assured the visual account of this episode from the life of Christ an unprecedented degree of veracity; it was also what lent it value as a commodity. Hunt sold *The finding of the Saviour in the temple* (**3**) to the engraver Gambart for the then gigantic sum of five thousand guineas. In conversation with Thackeray, Hunt records himself as describing his work precisely in terms of an industrial venture, like gold mining or importing commodities from the East:

Painting subject pictures . . . is an expensive profession, and after my experience of going to the East on a small capital, I feel obliged to postpone returning there for further work until I have a little money invested to bring me an income that will save me from daily fear that my means will be absorbed before my canvas has been turned into a picture. (Hunt, 1905, 2, p. 194)

In his written account of his experiences in the Holy Land, Hunt embellished and edited and, even in the primary document, wrote with an evident literary consciousness of his readership. The introduction of figures of speech and particularly the use of literary and biblical quotations also occurs in the processing of data into visual representation. Hunt's elaborately detailed depiction was placed in a frame of his own designing which underscores the exotic nature of the subject-matter. Nonetheless, the detail is itself contained in a perspective composition that was reassuringly Western and traditional. This careful balance of the strange and the familiar is undoubtedly one of the reasons for Hunt's

4 W. Holman Hunt, *The light of the world*

considerable commercial success.

When working on *The shadow of death* (**2**) in Jerusalem Hunt was pestered by local people who wanted to see the back of the painting because, they allegedly said, having seen Christ's face and Mary's back, they now wished to see Christ's back and Mary's face (Hunt, 1905, 2, p. 307). This is, of course, another account which stresses veracity, this time by a re-working of the popular accounts of paintings which were so real that humans and animals were deceived by them.[7] The Roman Catholic community in Jerusalem was forbidden to see the painting on account of this back view of Mary which was adjudged unworthy. Hunt says that he tried all ways to show Mary's face but was obliged in the end to depict her looking up to the shadow on the wall. What he does not say is that the figure echoes the kneeling maid in Titian's *Venus of Urbino*. The back view of a woman kneeling before a chest has an unmistakable resonance in Western art; the reference may be unconscious but it functions powerfully, nonetheless, endowing the work once again with an aura of tradition. The connection, once made, is also very disturbing, since in the taut semi-naked body of Christ Hunt has produced an alternative to one of the most familiar images of Western female eroticised nudity.

This suggestive allusiveness of imagery is a recurrent feature. Whereas what valorised Hunt's work as *religious* communication was the slavish pursuit of detail on site in the Middle East, in terms of iconography there is a very conspicuous slippage between secular and religious models that makes it difficult to categorise paintings within the traditional genre system. Where, for instance, should *The scapegoat* be placed? Is it an animal subject, a landscape with wild life or an allegorical history painting? Is *The Miracle of the holy fire* (**3**) a contemporary History painting or a Biblical painting, religious or ethnographic?

In 1848 Hunt had participated in an atheistic exercise in which Rossetti drew up a 'manifesto of our absence of faith in immortality, save in that perennial influence exercised by great thinkers and works' (Hunt, 1905, 1, p. 159). An easy disregard for religious and secular classification is discernible also in the way Hunt addressed the Middle East. The watercolour *Arab by a stream* might well be a study for an Old Testament figure but also replicates the pose familiar in Western art from Classical times and reproduced in British portraiture, most notably in Joseph Wright of Derby's portrait of Sir Brook Boothby reclining by a stream in his park, holding a copy of Rousseau (1781, Tate Gallery). *The afterglow . . .* works as a meaningful statement for a Western audience only through Western conventions of the pastoral. This demands an allegorised female figure of bounty detached from the documented 'realism' of her surroundings.[8]

Hunt saw the Middle East in terms of extreme polarities; he described the desert in sinister and contradictory terms: 'The mountains lie afar beautiful as precious stones but anear they are dry and scorched, the rose colour is the burnt ashes of the grate, the golden plain is the salt and naked sand and the sea is heavens own blue' (MS Ryl.). At the same time he declares his fear and loathing of the region's inhabitants. 'The horror of these arabs is that one cannot have anything to do with them without losing one's temper', he wrote in his diary. Writing to Thomas Combe, he referred to Egyptian women as 'dirty greasy eastern women', whom he would not allow 'near enough to me to hide the clear pink and white of clever-beautiful English girls' (MS Combe, 29 July 1854).

Hunt's self-proclaimed role as priest and warrior in the Middle East is also contradictory. 'I regard my occupation as somewhat akin to that of the priests', he wrote in his diary and, later, when suffering acutely from diarrhoea and tempted to abandon the project, 'I remembered that want of courage failed as much in such pursuits as mine as in war . . .' (Journal, MS Bodleian, Eng. lett. C296). The identification with these personae was undoubtedly a strategy for combating the fear and alienation that constantly assailed the artist. The members of the Pre-Raphaelite Brotherhood were interested in dreams but Hunt, during his Middle East journey of 1854, seems to have been (not surprisingly) in a state of considerable psychological disturbance and was not only dreaming vividly but was influenced by those dreams in his daytime actions. Right at the beginning of his journey he decided to curtail his stay in Paris because of the dreams of death that he was experiencing, induced, as he explains, by thinking of the history of Paris. At the Dead Sea on 22 November he wrote in his diary of his dreams and the intensity of his introspectiveness:

Last night I dreamed that I had just entered my brother-in-law's house, but that my youngest sister on coming downstairs could not see me. I confess that in my solitude these things affect me somewhat still I am glad even in such cases to have had the company of them who are a thousand [miles away]. (Journal, 22 Nov., MS Ryl.)

Fear of death, fear of exclusion and invisibility, fear of annihilation, all are – not surprisingly – central to Hunt's experiences during his 1854–55 travels. When Hunt came to transcribe into pictorial form the experiences he had witnessed with such disgust at the Church of the Holy Sepulchre in 1855 he produced (in The miracle of the Holy Fire (1)) what amounts to a visual encyclopaedia of racial types distributed over the canvas with an evenness that belies the wild abandon of the event that had so alarmed him. Landow's comparison with Frith's crowd scenes (as in *Derby day*, for example) is apposite but the event represented is, as I shall indicate, much more than 'a somewhat bizarre Easter eve rite' and the painting does not 'uneasily combine Hogarthian satire on the evils of superstition with the artist's desire to create an exotic bit of ethnographic, anthropological and historical fact' (Landow, 1983, pp. 471, 477). The key to the process of stabilization and control, the rendering safe, is the introduction into the lower right-hand corner of a European woman accompanied by an Arab servant. Like a figure of Charity, the mother shields her two children from the sight of the excesses which the viewer of the painting is being offered. Hunt published a description of the painting in 1900, including a key to all the figures; 9 and 10 are 'English mother and children' and 'Ayah of the same'.[9] The ambivalence of the artist in his role as ethnographer is enshrined in these figures. The device enabled Hunt to objectify the fear and aversion produced by the experience of those customs he was so intent on recording. The fact that the event was Christian – an intense and violent acting – out of scenes of the passion by Russian, Greek, Armenian, Albanian, Egyptian and Abyssinian pilgrims (as Hunt records in his description) – but controlled by the troops of Islam, lends it a powerful significance in colonial terms. Hunt could identify neither with pilgrim nor soldier but had to find a means of appropriating the occasion for a western Protestant gaze by absorbing it into a discourse of 'otherness'. In *The shadow of death* (2) no such device is available and the construction of European self as separate from the event in which it is also a participant does not occur. Rather the body of Christ becomes the site of struggle of the colonising brush, the place where the battle for space in the professional, historical, personal and geographical senses is fought.

So we return to the problem of how to represent Christ; here was the challenge of Hunt's career. Could he advance beyond *The light of the world* (4)? His subject involved the detailed study of the human body in affliction and pain. Work on this painting thus brought together for Hunt the fear of failure in his chosen profession as biblical painter in a major and innovative mode with the fear of death, disease and bodily suffering that he experienced daily whilst travelling in the Middle East. How to represent Christ was the point of challenge at which the ambiguities, conflicts and irresolutions, theological and personal, came together. It was, as we have established, a problem for the age; in the early 1860s the young Gerard Manley Hopkins began to write poetry which adduces the physicality of Christ and his world in tense celebration. The obligation laid on artists in the Protestant cause was a heavy one. As Charles Kingsley put it: 'In this day only can we reconcile the contradiction by which both Scripture and common sense talk of our bodies as at once not us and yet us' (Kingsley to Thomas Cooper, 19 June 1848, Kingsley, p. 72). If, as Leo Steinberg has argued, it is true that 'artists in the Renaissance were the only group within Christendom whose métier requiring them to plot every inch of Christ's body ... asking intimate questions that do not translate well into words', like whether Christ clipped his fingernails, how much more true was this for the nineteenth-century artist–ethnographer (Steinberg, p. 16). There were pictorial models in Counter-Reformation art but this manifestation was tainted with Roman Catholicism. A new pictorial solution was required.

Landow has argued convincingly for a typological approach to The Shadow of death (2), suggesting that this representation of Christ with uplifted hands not only appears to recapitulate Hunt's earlier abandoned Christ and the two Maries, itself probably derived from Dürer, but also embodies other types like Moses in his victory over the Amalekites.[10] What this explanation ignores is that we are drawn into this huge painting (it measures 214.2 × 168.2 cm) at the level of Christ's thighs through a sequence of severed forms, angular interruptions and cut-off spaces. If, as has been argued, we are meant to read the painting through the faceless Mary who, kneeling, looks up and sees the shadow of the cross on the wall, it does not work (Landow, 1979, p. 121). We are arrested by the gesture of Christ whose masochistically taut body, complete with sinews, body hair, sweat and dilated veins is offered up to us, its surfaces as disturbingly broken to the gaze as the chaotic fragmentation of the harshly-lit room in which he stands.

It has been demonstrated that spatial symmetry is essential to a person's narcissistic structure. 'The instinct of self-preservation deflects into the vertigo of the domination of space.' Lacan argues that fragmentation and mutilation is commonly the imago that represents 'the elective vector of aggressive intention' (Lacan, Écrits, p. 10).[11] The biblical–colonial project in which Hunt was engaged concerned a conquest of space both in the particular sense of his own itinerary and his own need to appropriate the 'other' foreign space he was depicting in order to be able to work day by day, and in the general sense of his being an Englishman. Space is also the primary mechanism for colonial discourse in painting, from the crowded harems of Delacroix and J. F. Lewis to the empty deserts of Hunt and Gérôme.

The peculiar crowding effects of Hunt's The finding of the Saviour in the temple (3) are achieved by contradictions between perspectival space (on which we have already remarked) and the lining-up of figures on the surface. The figure of the Christ child in this picture acquires authority not from larger dimensions – as in pre-Renaissance and non-naturalistic modes of representation – but by an equivalent contrivance whereby adults are reduced to child-height and deprived of space. In The Shadow of death (2), Christ's body is mapped in a way that the landscape glimpsed through the window can never be; public celebration of the body of the beloved Christ foregrounds violence as an inherent condition of that subjectivity on which Hunt's professional goal was predicated.

The fear of death that we have noted as an expression of Hunt's Middle East experience was anticipated in an early drawing, One step to the death bed. The sado-masochistic qualities of the representation of Christ's body in The shadow of death (and let us remember just how markedly it differs from that in The light of the world) register a move from the fear of death to fear of mutilation and damage to the body.[12] The affective nature of the painting goes beyond what we can explain by biblical history or typology. Whilst the term 'sado-masochistic' may point to an ahistorical judgement, it is the term that can most cogently invoke the obsessive depiction of the body's surface. Whilst not without compositional precedents as an image of Christ in agony, Hunt's attention to surface and his deployment of images of fragmentation are vividly out of key with the production of a seamless nudity, whether male or female, that was the norm in nine-teenth-century European academic painting. The exposed body in the painting is threatened by sharp instruments, the metaphorical 'body' of the carpenter's bench is effectively half-severed by a saw embedded in the wood, and the floor is covered with shavings like the littered detritus of crumbling skin and bone.

The cross that we see only as a shadow is, for Christ, not only his instrument of torture but – theologically and physically – also his support. The figure of Christ in Hunt's painting approximates most closely to an ancient crucifix where the wood has decayed and only Christ's stretched body remains, the cast of the limbs invoking the absent support. Take away the cross by accident of time or by intention and you have a twice-mutilated body which, lacking an essential limb, shocks by its deviancy, by its failure to fulfil expectations. The pose of Christ with uplifted arms then offers up its full range of ambiguities. Just as Hunt could slip easily from the devotion of the three Maries for the resurrected

Christ to the love of Porphyro and Madeline, so he presents a pose which can mean surrender in the moment of defeat or availability in a sexual sense. The ethnographer–artist's ambivalence towards the territory he colonises is configured as desire turned back upon itself; the body of Christ thus offers itself as the injured narcissistic body of self-identification, the body which is the object of desire and the site of damage, the colonial space that is to be occupied.

Notes

I would like to thank John Barrell, Joany Hichberger and Judith Bronkhurst for reading and commenting on this chapter.

1 Information concerning paintings by Hunt cited in this essay is given at the end of the chapter.

2 Sir John Gardner Wilkinson, *Modern Egypt and Thebes: being a description of Egypt, including the information required for travellers in that country*, 2 vols., London, 1843, new edition published in *Handbook for travellers*, 1847, eleven editions between 1843 and 1907; *The Architecture of ancient Egypt . . . with remarks on the early progress of architecture, etc.*, London, 1850; Edward William Lane, *An account of the manners and customs of the modern Egyptians*, 2 vols., London, 1836; eight editions between 1836 and 1906.

3 Sections of Hunt's diary (MS John Rylands Library, Eng. 1210, 1211) have been published by Judith Bronkhurst in Parris, p. 111, *passim*. I am grateful to Dr Bronkhurst for allowing me to see transcripts of those sections of Hunt's record that are retained overseas and for her most helpful advice on this essay; Hunt's letters to Thomas Combe, the Oxford publisher and close friend of the young Pre-Raphaelites, are cited by courtesy of the Bodleian Library, MS Eng. lett. C296; further material relating to Hunt's visit to the Middle East in 1870 is quoted courtesy of the Archives of the History of Art, the Getty Center for the History of Art and the Humanities, Santa Monica, California. Hereafter these MS sources will be referred to as Ryl., Combe, and Getty respectively.

4 *Pre-Raphaelitism and the Pre-Raphaelite Brotherhood* was largely written in the mid-1880s, parts were published in the *Contemporary review*, 1886 and 1887, the full account only appearing before the public in 1905.

5 Judith Bronkhurst has pointed out to me that the Fogg oil sketch was begun in 1870 but the painting in Liverpool was commenced in 1875, on the third visit.

6 Full explanations of the background details to all Hunt's Middle East paintings, which have been researched thoroughly, are to be found in Bennett, 1969 and in the entries in *The Pre-Raphaelites*. A definitive account is forthcoming in J. Bronkhurst's *Catalogue raisonné* to be published by Yale University Press.

7 E.g. Zeuxis's painting of a boy with grapes which were so realistically portrayed that birds flew in through the window to peck them. Pliny the Elder, *Natural history*, 35.

8 Various convincing suggestions have been made as to the pictorial source for this figure in published texts about the East. These are recorded by Judith Bronkhurst in *The Pre-Raphaelites*, no. 87. These models are, of course, themselves Western representations of the East and have to be taken in the context of the general point being made here.

9 *The Miracle of the holy fire in the Church of the Sepulchre at Jerusalem, painted by W. Holman-Hunt*, n.p., n.d. (1900); the only other Middle East painting in which a European presence is to be seen is *The lantern maker's courtship*, in the background to which a top-hatted man is seen about to strike an Arab.

10 Judith Bronkhurst has pointed out that the early studies for *Christ and the two Maries* suggest Hunt intended Christ's left arm to be outstretched; the Christ we now see was re-painted

in the 1890s. In this case we might suppose that the earlier painting was re-thought in relation to the later, confirming a thematic linkage.

11 The connection between paranoia, space and colonial discourse is most cogently defined by Homi Bhabha (p. 80): 'In the oscillation between aopocalypse and chaos, we see the emergence of an anxiety associated with the narcissistic vision and its two-dimensional space. It is an anxiety which will not abate because the empty third space, the *other* space of symbolic representation, at once bar and bearer of difference, is closed to the paranoid position of power. In colonial discourse, that space of the other is always occupied by an *idée fixe*: despot, heathen, barbarian, chaos, violence.'

12 Lacan points out that the fear of death, the absolute master, is subordinate to the fear of damage to one's own body (*Ecrits*, p. 28).

Works by Holman Hunt cited in text, listed in order of mention

The scapegoat, oil on canvas, 1856, Lady Lever Art Gallery; oil on canvas, 1854–55, Manchester City Art Galleries

The miracle of the Holy Fire, oil on canvas, 1893, Fogg Art Museum, Cambridge, Mass.

The shadow of death, oil on canvas, 1869–72, Leeds City Art Gallery, replica, 1873, Manchester City Art Galleries

Christ and the two Maries, oil on canvas, 1847, 1897, Art Gallery of Southern Australia, Adelaide

The lantern maker's courtship, oil on canvas, 1854–56, 1860–61, Birmingham Museum and Art Gallery

The afterglow in Egypt, oil on canvas, 1854, 1860–63, Southampton Art Gallery; oil on canvas, 1861, Ashmolean Museum, Oxford

The finding of the Saviour in the temple, oil on canvas, 1854–55, 1856–60, Birmingham Museums and Art Gallery

The triumph of the innocents, oil on linen, 1878, Walker Art Gallery, Liverpool

The light of the world, oil on canvas, 1853, Keble College, Oxford; oil on canvas, 1857, Manchester City Art Galleries

Arab by a stream, watercolour, 1854, Sheffield City Art Galleries

One step to the death bed, drawing, private collection, reproduced in *the Pre-Raphaelites*, no. 159

3

Reading The awakening conscience rightly
Kate Flint

Holman Hunt's *The awakening conscience* (5) exhibited at the Royal Academy summer exhibition of 1854, is a familiar work. It shows a girl who, sitting singing with her seducer, has suddenly been struck by alarm and remorse at the immoral position in which she finds herself. Even in describing it thus, I have turned the frozen moment on the canvas surface into a sequence, a narrative, the method most frequently employed by those contemporary commentators who treated the picture at any length.

The critic who commented in the most detail on the painting in 1854 was John Ruskin. Writing to *The Times* on 5 May 1854, he defended *The awakening conscience*: 'I am at a loss to know how its meaning could be rendered more distinctly, but assuredly it is not understood. People gaze at it in a blank wonder, and leave it hopelessly' (Ruskin, 12, p. 333). He made it clear that one should interpret the painting not as if it mimetically represented some incident from real life, but according to a *literary* model: this is apparent in his choice of verb: 'There is not a single object in all that room, common, modern, vulgar . . . but it becomes tragical, if rightly read' (p. 334). The question which I wish to address in this essay is 'What does "right reading" mean?' Is 'reading' here referring to an actual practice of deciphering, or is it being used more widely, as a metaphor for understanding? In what ways may we today usefully speak of 'reading' a mid-nineteenth-century picture, and how common a concept was it at the time? In particular, what discourses come into play when we consider the contemporary decipherment of the picture, and, indeed, is it possible to say what 'reading' *The awakening conscience* 'rightly' or 'wrongly' may entail?

Ruskin himself provides a detailed 'reading' of the painting, pointing to a single meaning which he believes to be encoded in each of the visual signifiers, amplified by Hunt's style:

That furniture so carefully painted, even to the last vein of the rosewood – is there nothing to be learnt from that terrible lustre of it, from its fatal newness; nothing there that has the old thoughts of home upon it, or that is ever to become a part of home? Those embossed books, vain and useless – they also new – marked with no happy wearing of beloved leaves; the torn and dying bird upon the floor; the gilded tapestry, with the fowls of the air feeding on the ripened corn; the picture above the fireplace with its single drooping figure – the woman taken in adultery; nay, the very hem of the poor girl's dress, which the painter has laboured so closely thread by thread, has story in it, if we think how soon its pure whiteness may be soiled with dust and rain, her outcast feet failing in the street; and the fair garden flowers seen in the reflected sunshine of the mirror – these also have their language:

'Hope not to find delight in us, they say,
For we are spotless, Jessy – we are pure' (p. 334)

May this, however, accurately be called a 'right reading'? There is one demonstrable error: the picture above the fireplace is actually an engraving of a work by Frank Stone, popularly known in its engraved form as *Cross Purposes*. Moreover, Ruskin's sudden assumption that the girl will be an outcast on the streets, whilst having some social foundation, fits oddly both with the painting's title, the interpretative hint offered by the star at the top of the frame and, if one gives weight to intentionality, with Hunt's comment on the picture: 'My desire was to show how the still small voice speaks to a human soul in the turmoil of life' (Hunt, 1905, 1, p. 347).

Both these observations by Ruskin emphasise how a critic's own subjectivity can easily become involved in the interpretation of a picture. But there is another danger. The fullness of the commentary risks coming to function as a substitute for the picture itself, inviting one to believe that the 'reading' is now closed. This, of course, can instantly be disproved in several ways: by looking at details which Ruskin's commentary fails to elucidate – the French clock on the piano, for example, represents Chastity binding Cupid; by considering artistic borrowings in the composition – George Landow has noted the similarity of the two figures to those in Dürer's *Young woman attacked by death (the ravisher)*: in each the girl struggles from the embrace of her suitor and reaches towards new life (Landow, 1979, p. 52). Ruskin's emphases could be replaced by later commentary, particularly that furnished by Frederick Stephens in the booklet he prepared, with Hunt's assistance, for the exhibition of the artist's works in 1860, when he stresses the social and economic implications of the scene, claiming the work 'might be said to have done not a little in calling attention to the class concerned in it. It showed the

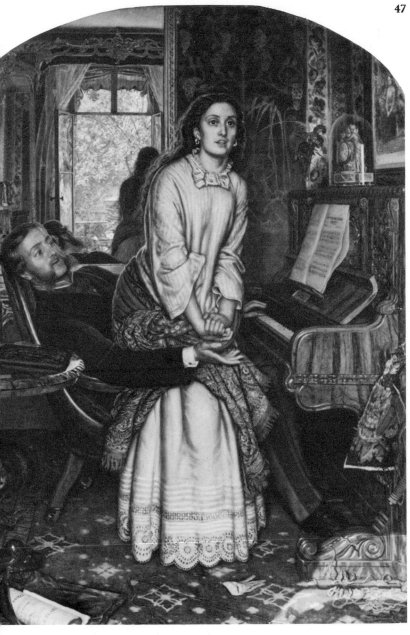

5 W. Holman Hunt, *The awakening conscience*

interior of one of those *maisons damnées* which the wealth of a seducer has furnished for the luxury of a woman who has sold herself and her soul to him' (Stephens, p. 32) – indeed, in a Pre-Raphaelite quest after accuracy, Hunt hired for the purpose a typical *maison de convenance*, Woodbine Villa in St John's Wood.

But what interests us here is not Ruskin's accuracy, but his method. What concept of reading was he applying to the painting?

Ruskin wrote extraordinarily little about reading, considering his perennial concern with perception and interpretation. Like other forms of cultural activity, he regarded its practice as organically indivisible from moral effect, writing in *Fors Clavigera*, 85: 'The sense, to a healthy mind, of being strengthened or enervated by reading, is just as definite and unmistakable as the sense, to a healthy body, of being in fresh or foul air' (Ruskin, 29, p. 322). Reading, indeed, was literal consumption, a bodily appetite, and thus to be controlled: 'Gluttonous reading is a worse vice than gluttonous eating.' 'It should not be indulged in for pleasure but use' (Ruskin, 28, pp. 501–2). 'Of kings' treasuries', the first of the *Sesame and lilies* lectures, where Ruskin gives his most sustained advice about reading, is, however, more to our purpose when considering how he viewed the method, rather than the results, of reading. Strangely, he does not advocate a synthetic model of reading, but rather, would have one break down the composite effect of paragraph, of sentence, of phrase: 'You must get into the habit of looking intensely at words, and assuring yourself of their meaning, syllable by syllable – nay, letter by letter' (Ruskin, 18, p. 64). This 'accuracy', he maintains, leads to true education, by which he means, among other things, understanding the layers of linguistic sediment which go to make up our language: 'Nearly every word in your language has been first a word of some other language' (p. 68). It is easy to see how this theory transfers both to his method of deciphering *The awakening conscience*, and indeed to the composition of the painting.

We can trace this not just through the moral overtones Ruskin picks up through pointing out the signifying systems to which the fluttering bird or the wall decorations allude, but also through this painted text's incorporation of literary texts. Hunt's work relies on the fact that his audience would themselves recognise the literature whose words have helped awaken the thoughts of the woman. At the piano, she has been singing Thomas Moore's 'Oft in the stilly night', itself about nostalgia for past forms of affection:

Oft in the stilly night,
    Ere slumber's chain has bound me,
Fond memory brings the light
    Of other days around me;
        The smiles, the tears,
        Of boyhood's years,
The words of love then spoken;
    The eyes that shone,
    Now dimm'd and gone,
The cheerful hearts now broken.

This theme of the power of song to stimulate bitter regret and to trouble the conscience is over-determined: the music for Tennyson's 'Tears, idle tears', from *The princess*, set to music by Hunt's friend Edward Lear in 1853, lies on the floor:

Tears, idle tears, I know not what they mean,
Tears from the depth of some divine despair
Rise in the heart, and gather to the eyes,
In looking on the happy autumn-fields,
And thinking of the days that are no more.

Moreover, whilst the popular title of the Stone engraving, *Cross purposes*, suggests a love quarrel, the female figure portrayed is, according to the 1840 Academy catalogue, that of Annot Lyle, in Walter Scott's *The legend of Montrose*, moving the heart of Allan M'Anley by her song. A further, more encoded reference to reading – indeed, paralleling Ruskin's advocated method of reading – is incorporated in the picture by the books on the table, the right-hand one of which, with a beautiful papier-maché moulded cover, very closely resembles Henry Noel Humphrey's *The origin and progress of the art of writing*. Rather than alluding to education – for Judith Bronkhurst has suggested that the book's presence refers to the fact that at the time Annie Miller posed for the girl in the picture, Hunt was ensuring that she follow a two-year plan of education (*The Pre-Raphaelites*, no. 58) – Hunt draws our attention to the question of writing. Humphrey's book is a scholarly work which traces the forms of hands from hieroglyphics to modern scripts. The description Humphreys gives of how writing originated considers it as a form of signification similar to that employed by Hunt in this picture, and looked for, anachronistically, by Ruskin in his description of the ideal reading process. Writing's origins, claimed Humphreys, lay 'not in an attempt to note by marks or signs the sounds of language, but by pictorial imitations to represent objects, and by their modifications, to express abstract ideas' (p. 176).

But – judging by recorded reactions to the picture – these internal clues to interpretation went unremarked. In his letter, Ruskin commented that to many people, 'the careful rendering of the inferior details in this picture cannot but be at first offensive', and this reaction is certainly borne out by contemporary reviews. The *Globe*'s critic, for example, complained that 'every flower in the carpet, every bit of gilding in the clock and cornice, every spray of foliage outside the window, are represented with equal minuteness in Mr. Hunt's picture. It almost reminds us of the marriageable maiden's complaint: "It used to be females fust, but now it's furnitur." The accessories detract from the principles.' This lack of discrimination in detail in *The awakening conscience* was contrasted with the style of one of the most popular pictures shown that year, E. M. Ward's *Last sleep of Argyle*: '. . . the Earl of Argyle's bible, watch, etc.', said the *Globe*, 'deserve the careful painting [Ward] has given them, because they help the story, and swell the pathos of the situation. Had those highly painted foreground objects had no such function, to have forced them upon the eye would have been to spoil the picture' (29 April 1854, p. 2). Old standards were threatened by Hunt's picture: Reynolds's maxim, for example, that 'the whole of beauty consists, in my opinion, in being able to get above singular forms, local customs, particularities, and details of every kind'.

It was not that the English public was entirely unused to 'reading' pictures in this way, although Hunt's density of incorporated allusions was rare. The *Globe*, again, was perspicacious enough, at least, to recognise that 'Mr. Hunt follows in Hogarth's footsteps': Hogarth, who furnished his interiors with pictures and signs to be read, who was popular in the mid-nineteenth century and whose methods were adopted by many mid-Victorian artists. Pictorial fictions and narrative text came notably together in Hunt's own time in the illustrations Hablot K. Browne (more commonly known as 'Phiz') provided for Dickens's novels. In the illustration accompanying Chapter 22 of *David Copperfield* (**7**), for example, we are shown Martha's kneeling position paralleled with the pose of Mary Magdalene anointing Christ's feet, in the picture over the fireplace – suggesting future remorse and forgiveness – and Emily beneath a print of Eve and the serpent, prefiguring her fall. Being asked to pick up an allusion in a painting was not a novelty for the Academy public: they had been invited to do so, for example, in relation to a similar subject in Richard Redgrave's *The outcast* (exhibited in 1851), where the picture on the wall is of Abraham banishing Hagar and her illegitimate son Ishmael. Whilst Ruskin's careful explication was unique among responses to this picture in 1854, his method of taking a painted

moment and turning it into a moral narrative was readily adopted by
Tom Taylor, in particular, most obviously in his 'reading' of the central
painting of the triptych by Hunt's friend Augustus Egg, *Past and present*
(1858), where the wife:

lies prostrate before her heart-stricken partner, who holds the letter, the evidence
of her treachery, in his hand. Their two children look up from their amusement of
card castle-building at the sound of her fall. Their card castle has a French novel
[by Balzac] for its foundation – a Hogarthian indication of the source of their
mother's perversion, a mode of pointing a moral carried still further by the
'goodly apple rotten at the core' on the table, and the pictures of Adam and Eve
driven out of Paradise and Stanfield's 'Abandoned' on the walls'. (*The Times*, 22
May 1858, p. 9)

In *Inquiries into the fundamentals of aesthetics*, Stefan Morawski remarks that
'quotes are a proof if not a badge of learning' (p. 341). In employing these
visual references in the first place, and in drawing attention to them in
reviews, artists and critics are assuming a certain cultural awareness
among their readers. It is a mode of explication which fosters their sense
of a common cultural and social identity. Morawski coins the term
'paraquotation' to describe those types of interpolation 'with a stimula-
tory–amplificatory function' (pp. 355–6) and argues that not only is
paraquotation a means adopted particularly by artists with theses to
prove, as in the case of Hunt or Egg, but habitually accumulates 'in art
when the boundaries between it and other forms of social consciousness
become vague' (p. 359). The connection between 'readable' pictures on
the one hand, and the combination of elaborate yet resolved plots,
emphasis on the moral aspect of cause and effect, and the solid specificity
of detail embraced by the mid-Victorian novel on the other, scarcely
seems accidental. It is particularly tempting to draw a parallel between
The awakening conscience and Wilkie Collins's *Basil* (1852). Hunt saw his
friend Collins regularly during his painting of this picture, and there is a
strong resemblance between the interior of Woodbine Villa and North
Villa, Hollyoake Square, just north of Regent's Park, where Basil's inamo-
rata, daughter of the owner of a large linen draper's shop, lived; where
'Everything was oppressively new', with 'paper on the walls, with its
gaudy pattern of birds, trellis-work and flowers', its 'round rosewood
table' with picture books on it: 'not one leaf even of the music on the
piano was dogs-eared or worn' (p. 61), and where, later in the novel, Basil
sees Margaret in a 'paroxysm of passion', with her black eyes flashing
through her tears, her lips parted as she gasped for breath, one hand
clenched on the mantelpiece, the other convulsively clasping her dress

as the cat kills her pet bird (p. 134). Whilst direct collusion is unprovable, we can, importantly, say that painter and novelist shared a common mode of looking at both furniture and gesture, regarding both as social and moral indicators.

Hunt himself later claimed that he had been influenced by one of Collins's literary friends in his early plans for the painting, recalling how in searching for a material counterpart to the spiritual message in *The light of the world* (4), showing 'How the appeal of the spirit of heavenly love calls a soul to abandon a lower life', he thought of old Peggotty's search after the fallen Emily in *David Copperfield*. Yet he came to the conclusion

that the instinctive eluding of pursuit by the erring one would not coincide with the willing conversion and instantaneous resolve for a higher life which it was necessary to emphasise.

While recognising this, I fell upon the text in Proverbs, 'As he taketh away a garment in cold weather, so is he that singeth songs to a heavy heart.' (Hunt, 1905, 2, p. 429)

The awakening conscience was designed to be 'read' in the light of two further scriptural texts printed in the catalogue: Ecclesiastes 14:18: 'As of the green leaves on a thick tree some fall and some grow, so is the generation of flesh and blood'; and Isaiah 35:3,4: 'Strengthen ye the feeble hands, and confirm ye the tottering knees; say ye to the faint-hearted be ye strong: fear ye not, behold your God.' Like Egg's *Past and present* triptych, it was intended to be comprehended alongside, if not in sequence with, Hunt's other exhibited work of 1854, *The light of the world*, where Christ knocks on even the most firmly shut door of the confirmed sinner. Such a dialogue, however, was hard for the exhibition visitor to appreciate, since *The awakening conscience* (5) was hung in the Middle Room, *The light of the world* (4) in the West Room.

It is possible to construct further, more tenuous types of reading sequences in which to place *The awkening conscience*, in which 'reading' really does become a metaphor for 'understanding within a certain determined context'. One can, for example, place it in a line with Hunt's other Academy works dealing with the subject of straying. First, *The hireling shepherd* (shown 1852), an obvious pastoral seduction with moral overtones of Christ's flock in need of spiritual guidance. The lines from *King Lear* which accompanied it in the catalogue:

Sleepest or wakest thou, jolly shepherd?
   Thy sheep be in the corn;
And, for one blast of thy minikin mouth,
   Thy sheep shall take no harm

connect directly with the wall decoration in The awakening conscience, of which Stephens wrote in 1860: 'They bear a vineyard, in which corn is mingled with the vine' (imagery used by Hunt in his 1850 RA exhibit, *A converted British family sheltering a Christian missionary* . . . to symbolise, Hunt said 'the civilising effect' of Christianity): 'birds destroy the grapes of the latter, while at the foot sleeps a boy-guardian, whose horn, fallen from his hand, indicates neglected duty' (p. 34) *Our English coasts*, 1852 (*strayed sheep*) (shown 1853) does not just show actual and metaphorical flocks, but the absence of coastal defences endangers more than sheep: the coastline is vulnerable from France, the date in the title and the summer season in the painting alluding to the topicality: this was the time at which the Militia bill was being discussed in Parliament.

The awakening conscience may be placed in a further sequence: that of pictures with similar titles. In 1849, Richard Redgrave showed an *Awakened conscience*: a formal, classical Italian pastoral, 'in which is seen a man admonished by an angel. The wine cup is by his side, he looks at it with a shudder' (*Art journal*, June 1849, p. 172), the catalogue reader being reminded that wine 'biteth like a serpent, and sinneth like an adder' (Proverbs 23: 31), the language suggesting sin's origin in the sexual fall. Thomas Brooks showed an *Awakened conscience* the year before Hunt, with the epigraph in the catalogue:

> There was a time, thou blessed child!
> When young, and haply pure as thou,
> I look'd and pray'd like thee – but now –

Precisely what is going on in this crowded cottage interior (**6**), what has befallen the man, woman and child who are grouped by the door is hard to decipher. In the light of contemporary silence about how to 'read' Hunt's painting, the comment on Brooks's work in the *Athenaeum* – 'the imagination is not taxed very greatly to read the common-place story' (28 May 1853) – indicates how unintelligible certain lines of Victorian social narrative have become for us.

All the types of reading offered so far, however, return our attention back to The awakening conscience and its painter. As well as examining Hunt's creative method, we have been acquiescing to the notion of the inscribed, ideal reader, engaged in a self-conscious sense-making activity, observing, selecting, formulating concepts from the accumulation of objects in the canvas, and threading them together into a plausible narrative. Of course, given the unavoidable programmatic references which the painting contains, we have already had to take

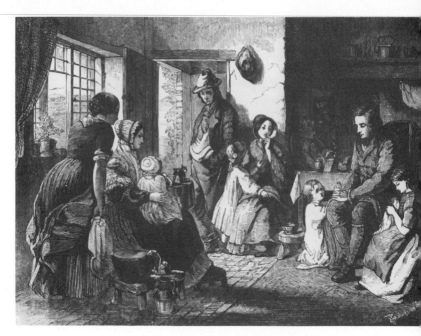

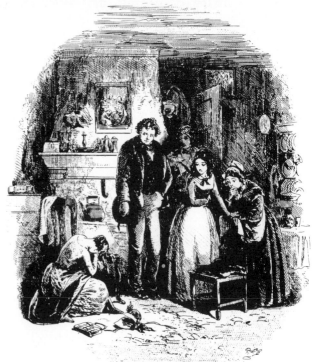

notice of the social codes to which it alludes. But this foregrounding of text rather than contexts by and large keeps our study within the terms of traditional art history. In an important way, we are still dehistoricising *The awakening conscience*, removing it from its immediate cultural contexts, its reception by *actual* readers, if we may call them that, in the midst of 1530 other exhibits at the 1854 Academy exhibition. I want to argue that 'right reading' – then or now – involves the acknowledgement of the way in which the painting's power to communicate rests to a large extent on its incorporation, and manipulation, of these social codes. But to do this profitably will involve more than centring on the individual work: it means abandoning what Stephen Bann has termed 'the debilitating assumption that a strict archival method, coupled with an interpretative *open sesame* which enables us to convert paintings into moral, social or political texts, will reveal to us all that needs to be known about visual representation' (Bann, p. 28). Rehanging it, as it were, in that exhibition, seeing how it was written about in the midst of other paintings – if, indeed, it was written about at all – will enable us not to use the reception of other works to further our understanding of Hunt's painting; rather, foregrounding *The awakening conscience* can become a means to lever open the whole way in which art was looked at and interpreted in the mid 1850s. This involves considering its relationship to other representations of social narrative, of cause and effect, which would have been available to those considering the before and after of this supposed arrested moment of 'awakening'.

I have deliberately not yet emphasised the particular importance which *The awakening conscience* has come to assume in recent years as a text in the Fallen Woman issue, notably in the writing of Lynda Nead and Helene Roberts (Nead, 1984; Roberts, pp. 48–51). The painting has inevitably been seen alongside such works as Rossetti's *Found* and Egg's *Past and present*. This last work, showing sexual transgression taking place within a family, apparently allows far less scope for the idea of rescuing the woman from her moral downfall to enter into the chain of images with which we are presented. Nonetheless Hunt, writing in 1864 of this very set of paintings, criticised the inevitability with which Egg invested the woman's descent: 'it is by no means', he said, 'a matter of course when a woman falls that she should die in misery. ... Indeed the adultress often reaps reward rather than punishment for her sin; and therefore the painter of this series should have shown how it was that his heroine suffered her punishment so directly. Hogarth left no gap in his

6 Thomas Brooks, *The awakened conscience*
7 Phiz, *Martha*, illustration to Dickens's *David Copperfield*

histories' (Hunt, Egg, p. 57). In *The awakening conscience*, the blame arguably falls ultimately on the woman as well as on the man since it is she who is shown to be in need or in reach of redemption rather than her seducer: Hunt, however, was himself well aware of this implied double moral standard. Edward Lear wrote to him on 12 October 1853: 'I think with you that it is an artificial lie that a woman should so suffer and lose all, while he who led her [to] do so encounters no share of evil from his acts' (*The Pre-Raphaelites*, no. 58). Whilst some fiction of the period, especially Elizabeth Gaskell's *Ruth* (1853), tried to relocate the blame, among visual representations, only Ford Madox Brown's unfinished – unsaleable? – *Take your son, sir*, 1856, attempts such a redressal, the seducer's figure appearing in the mirror which haloes the woman's head. Despite Hunt's verbal and visual attempts to query the inevitability in factual terms of a commonly-perceived sequence, Egg's representation of the fate of the 'fallen woman', married or unmarried, unquestionably fitted the popular stereotype. W. R. Greg, in 1850, spoke of such a decline: 'The career of these women is a brief one; their downward path a marked and inevitable one ... They are almost never rescued; escape themselves they cannot' (Greg, p. 454). A similar narrative model is still being offered, ten years later, in a piece entitled 'The downward course of ruin' in *The magdalen's friend and female homes intelligencer* (1860), where the helper of prostitutes is urged to tell the finely-dressed woman that:

her baronet patron will inevitably cast her off when his passions have been jaded; bid her prepare for a rapid descent from West-end brilliance to the gloom, dirt and squalor of a back slum; shew her, as in a prophetic mirror, her own countenance at thirty-six years of age, pale, wan, thin, hideous with disease and hunger, her form attenuated, clad in vermin-crowded rags, stretched palsied by famine on the naked boards, lifted into a cab, borne to the pauper's house, and there, in the very gateway of an abode more gaunt and cheerless than a prison, taken out stark dead. (p. 55)

Such narratives were directly challenged by the promise of moral salvation held out by *The awakening conscience* (**5**). The painting's suggestion that the downward path might well be arrested or reversed provides one obvious explanation – in addition to the nature of this contemporary subject in the first place – why many contemporary reviewers found it hard to write about.

But to what extent was this stress on the discourse of sexuality present in the conscious reaction of the Victorian exhibition visitor? How conscious was the repression which took place, excluding, by and large, any extended discussion of the painting's sexual implications from the notices of the exhibitions? When one looks around the exhibition, the tacit contrast between this painting and other representations of womanhood is conspicuous. The preceding work in the catalogue, Charles Baxter's vapid, sub-Reynoldsian *Love me, love my dog*, showing an adolescent girl clasping a King Charles spaniel, illustrates this instantly. So do two works which reviewers very frequently mentioned before *The light of the world* (**4**) as laudable examples of Christian art: first, the secular motherhood and devotional almsgiving in W. C. T. Dobson's *The charity of Dorcas*, and second, W. E. Frost's acclaimed allegory, *Chastity* (**8**), accompanied in the catalogue with the apposite lines from *Comus*:

> So dear to Heaven is saintly chastity,
> That when a soul is found sincerely so,
> A thousand liveried angels lackey her,
> Driving far off each thing of sin and guilt.

The only other representation of a fall from innocence would seem to be an unevenly received work by James Sant, *The children in the wood*, illustrating the verses:

> The wood is thick with melody – the way
>   Leads to delight, where'er their pathway goes;
> And through the golden hours of autumn's day
>   A new enchantment every footprint shows.
>
> Till by a sudden spell together bound,
>   In terror ice drops, full their pulses beat;
> Ah! woe which parts not till their world be o'er,
>   They rustle death beneath their infant feet,
> And with these blossoms dropped upon the ground
>   The flowers of life have left their grasp for evermore.

Yet, despite these allegorical overtones, the overall emphasis is on a sentimentalised version of conventional gender roles, Sant unequivocally showing a brave little boy supporting his faltering companion. Turning to other contemporary subjects, flirtation is a perfectly acceptable topic in Frank Stone's *The old, old story*, provided it is removed to an idealised version of the Breton peasantry and takes place outdoors, away from the carefully furnished bourgeois interior which in Hunt's painting approaches too nearly the appearance of a fashionable middle-class home: 'Just the room one might choose for the happy, early days, with the clinging wife of our youth' (*Magdalen's friend*, 1862, p. 266). Should courtship take place indoors, it is advisable that the couple should be under at least minimal surveillance, as in Rebecca Solomon's *The governess* – a different sort of protest picture

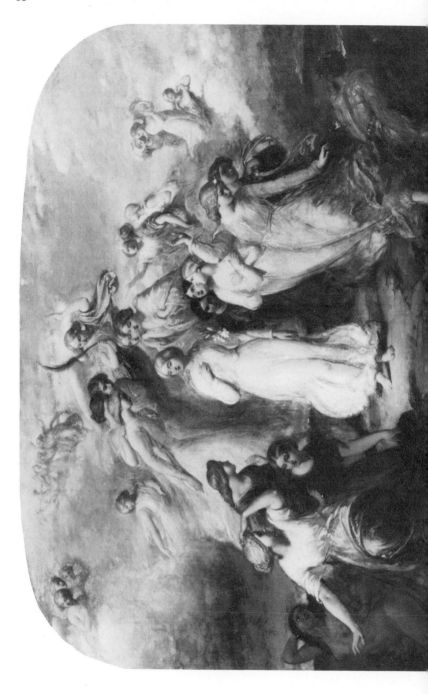

against the lot of women (Edmund and Suzanne McCormick Collection, USA). Exhibited with two lines from Martin Tupper's *Proverbial Philosophy* – 'Ye too, the friendless, yet dependent, that find neither home nor lover,/Sad imprisoned hearts, captive to the net of circumstance' – it seems to show the governess engaged in her duties whilst to her left, her employer – like her, in mourning – is flirting pleasantly with his potential second wife. Male and female sexuality are underscored by the language of the flowers outside the open door, where foxglove intertwines with lily. That the piano could play a crucial part in the iconography of Victorian eroticism, providing both physical proximity in the duet and the potential for the transportative power of music, is indicated not just by Hunt and Solomon but by its frequent presence in the fiction of the time (Burgan). Moreover, the dangerous affective power of music was a current commonplace in medical literature. Thomas Laycock, in *A treatise on the nervous diseases of women* (1840) quoted a Dr J. J. Johnson's comment that 'the stimulus of music is of a very subtle and diffusible nature, and the excitement which it produces in the nervous system is of a peculiar character, by no means generally understood' (p. 141), while E. J. Tilt in *On the preservation of the health of women at the critical periods of life* (1851) reiterated these sentiments, and, especially, warned against young ladies visiting the opera, because of the powerful combination of words, music and scenery – precisely the factors which seem to be operative in Hunt's painting.

Sexual morality was not just regarded as a domestic issue. Indeed, the perceived relationship between individual and national morality was widely discussed around the time that the 1854 Royal Academy exhibition opened in London. Though no critic seems to have taken the opportunity to place Hunt's painting in this wider context, it may be considered as one additional factor which ensured that its subject matter would be regarded as dubious. The private view was on Friday 28 April: on Wednesday of that week, England had formally entered the Crimean War, an event marked by a national Day of Humiliation (the revival of a practice from the Napoleonic wars), when shops, mills, factories, businesses and markets shut, and services were held throughout the country, which combined reference in the widely-reported sermons to the value of the family and the potential plight of widows and orphans with collections for soldiers' wives. As the editorial in the *Daily news* put it, this was a public manifestation of 'setting our house in order, and arranging our affairs, and clearing our

8 W. E. Frost, *Chastity*

hearts and minds, before going out to fight in a good cause' (26 April, p.
4), and this included, as in the sermon preached at St Pancras's Church,
condemnation of corruptors of innocence and stylised lamentation at
the moral condition of England:

How many drunkards disgraced our thoroughfares! how many harlots infested
our streets! . . . how many children grew up in the midst of us, from infancy to
youth, and from youth to manhood, without any knowledge of these principles
which might preserve the one sex from fraud and violence, and the other from
infamy and shame. (Daily news, 27 April, p. 6)

Moreover, sexual habits were being discussed in the press, since 3 May
saw the defeat for the badly put together bill by Mr Bowyer aimed at the
repression of adultery. Yet, whilst this is a context of debate which we
may reconstruct, the fact remains that no contemporary observer seems
to have chosen to make connections between acutely contemporary
issues and the pictures on display.

Only three critics of 1854 besides Ruskin seem to have gone very far at all
towards placing the subject – let alone the detail – of The awakening
conscience within a wider narrative framework. The first of these might
plausibly be termed a 'wrong' reading, if an interesting one. The New
monthly magazine believed the canvas to represent a tiff between a brother
and a sister, submerging socially forbidden eroticism behind a situation
involving legitimate, unspoken heterosexual connection:

The cause of this emotion, of this contrast between the pair, is explained in an
epigraph below the picture, which runs, as well as we can remember, thus: 'As he
who taketh away a garment in cold weather, so is he who asketh songs of a heavy
heart.' The lady looks not only as if she had been asked to sing at a wrong
moment, but as if one of her garments had actually been taken from her, for the
expression on her countenance is that of one who is shivering dreadfully. (May
1854, p. 49)

Writing at greater length, and with more understanding, the Athenaeum's reviewer introduces this picture as being 'drawn from a very dark
and repulsive side of modern domestic life . . . treated . . . with a great,
though mistaken depth . . . enigmatic [my italics] in its title . . . understood
by few of the exoteric visitors'. Anticipating the misrecognition of the
New monthly magazine, he confirms bluntly that though 'Innocent and
unenlightened spectators suppose it to represent a quarrel between a
brother and a sister: it literally represents the momentary remorse of a
kept mistress' (6 May 1854, p. 561). Having been so explicit, he is free to
place it in the context of other cultural representations of unsanctionable
sexuality: Hood, 'the author of "The Bridge of Sighs" could not have

conceived a more painful-looking face', and he continues: 'The sentiment is that of the Ernest Maltravers school, – to those who have an affinity for it, painful – and to those who have not, repulsive.' He is referring back to Bulwer-Lytton's ultimately moral tale of a young man whose life goes downhill once he's accidentally severed from a happy love affair. Bulwer-Lytton's novel, though, was published in 1837, Hood's poem in 1844, but no reviews seem prepared to stress the direct contemporaneity of the painting by relating it to, say, Elizabeth Gaskell's Ruth, which came out the previous year, or to a novel of the previous month, Lady Bulwer-Lytton's Behind the scenes, which dealt with the sexual double standards of an MP, or, indeed, to Basil. Moreover, my other example of criticism which puts this work in the discourses of contemporary sexuality may be unreliable in its moral vehemence, coming from Punch, writing, Janus-like, condemnatory on the one hand yet enjoying voyeurism under the guise of moralism on the other. The critic is not unsophisticated, au fait with the most useful model for getting the image to yield up its meaning, bidding us to remember Hogarth, who 'gives us pictures which are books'. Some claim that Hunt's picture's 'moral is obscure and his story unintelligible', but this critic seems determined to do what they fail to do and speak the unspeakable. The Spectator's correspondent – one of the painting's admirers – may be circumlocutory, calling the subject a 'painful one' without ever telling us quite what it is, euphemistically fumbling for words as he speaks of the woman's 'fashionable "protector" ' (27 May 1854, p. 567), but Punch goes straight to the point, commanding Hunt:

Tell us more home-truths. Set us face to face with our great sins again and again. Still paint our MAGDALENES, scared by the still small voice amid their bitter splendours, mocked in their misery by the careless smiles and gay voices of their undoers.
   Which of us is not better for that presentation of the woman waking from the dream of sin, meant not for the tempters only, but for the sisters of the tempted and the fallen? Why should our Exhibition lift up no voice to brand abominations against which the hard stones of our streets cry aloud, night after night? (3 June 1854, p. 229)

   It is notoriously difficult, however, to determine whether the silences and gaps of other critics are deliberate evasions, or whether, for a variety of reasons, the painting simply did not strike them as forcefully as it does us today. The Morning chronicle called The awakening conscience 'an absolutely disagreeable picture', failing to express its meaning either through composition or through details, yet since the only particular which it mentions is the fact that 'the mirror behind the figure is . . . a mere piece of intricacy without any good or valuable effect' (29 April 1854, p. 5), it is hard to tell whether the critic is reacting against the subject matter or not picking it up. Ruskin's letter to The Times is not, in fact, a correction of a 'wrong reading' in that paper but provides its readers with the painting's first discussion, since all they learnt on 29 April was that 'Mr Hunt . . . is indeed materially present in the gallery, but his spirit is most inadequately represented by the figure of the Redeemer, entitled the "Light of the World" ' (p. 12). The Morning post noted with relief on the same date that 'Pre-Raphaelite feeling, as a general mania' seemed to be 'on the wane'. Continuing these metaphors of mental disease, it claimed that there were still many 'confirmed individual cases to register, which being a disagreeable task, we postpone the examination of them to a future day' (29 April 1854, p. 6), but never in fact did so. The Daily news, expressing far more enthusiasm for Pre-Raphaelitism generally, lamented the absence of Millais, commended The light of the world (4) for its 'deep tenderness of sentiment – perfect beauty of form and colour and honesty of execution' (29 April 1854, p. 2), but pays no attention to Hunt's other work. One response to the fact that Hunt's painting was so little discussed in terms of its sexual subject-matter is to regard this as a clear example of the repression of sexual reference, at least in the official discourses of art criticism which accompanied the exhibition. But the fact that we learn from the Illustrated London news that, by 13 May, ' "the Awakening Conscience" of this clever painter is now familiarly known as "the Loose Lodging" ' (p. 438), undermines this, reminding us that whilst we may be able to recover the formal language of art criticism, there will be gaps between this and the way the painting's subject evidently entered popular discussion.

Moreover, the examples taken from printed reviews betray an overriding concern to link the painting in with an entirely different form of controversy: the debate about Pre-Raphaelite style, brightness, and superabundance of 'ugly' detail which had been so prominent in criticisms of the previous three Academies, and which represented a tendency which many critics were delighted to proclaim a brief passing phase, since this year there was no Millais, no Rossetti, no Brown: only Hunt's two pictures and an unremarkable Charles Collins, Thought of Bethlehem. Furthermore, more material factors must have had their part to play. Measuring 30 by 22 in. The awakening conscience was not a conspicuously commanding canvas – unlike Daniel Maclise's much written about Strongbow's marriage with the Princess Ida, which took up nearly one side of the middle room; 'next in point of conspicuousness' was Ward's *Last sleep of Argyle*, and then the undoubted popular success of the year, Frith's *Life at the sea-side*, which 'constantly attracted a little crowd', admired for its vivaciousness and its ability to mirror the middle-class public back to itself: 'a consummation of a hundred epitomes', the *Art journal* called it, before going on to invent some of the life-histories it contains (June 1854, p. 161). The fourth among this group of easily visible and popular pictures was Landseer's uncertainly received and unfinished *Royal sports on hill and loch*, the largest of all his royal commissions. This was a work which, claimed the *Daily news*, had to take precedence in a critique of the Exhibition through loyalty to the Monarch: other pictures very much took their chances according to the personal preferences of critics, the artists they knew or admired, the time in which they had to view the exhibition and the number of visits they could make: *The awakening conscience* (**5**) was just one among very many paintings which was amply noticed by some and passed over hastily by others. The picture itself did not have – again according to the *Illustrated London news* – a conspicuously good place awarded it by the hanging committee, and it would be good to discover more about this: how high was it? How legible? This, indeed, raises a problem about the readability of detail in Victorian exhibition painting: how can one determine the effect of something designed to be read as a contribution to a social, public issue when these very details, unless reproduced in an engraving, were virtually illegible except in a domestic setting or hung low on the wall?

In 1854 many critics considered that there were many good pictures, few really excellent ones. As the *Daily news* remarked: 'The present exhibition is – in short – a chapter in the collected works of the Academy; like one of those heavier chapters which we meet with at times even in the writings of the most brilliant novelists' (29 April 1854, p. 2). This functions as a means of returning, finally, to the part which the language of 'reading' played in the general criticism of the exhibition, and the way in which its employment militated against the type of reading which Ruskin had in mind.

Plenty of comparisons between written and painted texts were made by critics reviewing this, as other RA exhibitions. At a time when poetry unmistakably held a higher cultural status than fictional prose, it could be invoked in praise, as when the *Daily news*'s critic commends the concentrated beauty of effect in Stanfield's *View of the Pie du Midi d'Ossan*: 'the sentiment of the scene, and of the figures – human and animal – by which it is tenanted, is one – one through the fusing influence of imagination.

The picture is a poem!' (29 April 1854, p. 2). On the other hand, those pictures which are described as telling stories tended to be genre scenes, domestic moments, paintings much more likely to entertain or to point an obvious moral than to engage the interpretative faculties deeply. But at the same time, it is worth noting the widespread contemporary anxiety about the effects of prose reading, especially on women, considered to be more impressionable, more readily influenced consumers of fiction than their male counterparts (Flint). Ruskin was voicing a commonplace when he claimed in *Sesame and Lilies* that the best novel is a risk 'if, by its excitement, it renders the ordinary course of life uninteresting, and increases the morbid thirst for useless acquaintance with scenes in which we shall never be called upon to act' (Ruskin, 18, p. 129). At a time when even Gaskell's own daughters were forbidden *Ruth*, and *David Copperfield* was widely considered unsuitable reading for girls, *The awakening conscience* brought a private subject openly, dangerously, within a less controllable sphere than that of family reading.

Ruskin took up *The awakening conscience* again in 1856, in volume III of *Modern painters*. He wrote of how painting was beginning 'to take its proper position beside literature', artists coming to abandon the role of chronicler in favour of inventing the stories they paint. But despite the fact that I have been citing Ruskin's guide through *The awakening conscience* as an example of narrative approach, synthesising the details he dissects into a moral, rather than a compositional unity, Ruskin too obeyed an allegiance to traditional hierarchies of value. He differentiated between Hunt and those who painted 'merely the outward verities of passing events': the latter, if they 'worked worthily of their mission would become, properly so called, historical or narrative painters', whilst Hunt and his peers were designated by Ruskin, because of their faculties of originality, invention and feeling, '*poetical* painters' (Ruskin, 5, pp. 126–7). He cited Hunt's work as a laudable example of this, helping to launch, as a later influential art critic, R. A. M. Stevenson put it in 1886: '. . . the confusion between literary aims or conceptions and those proper to the plastic arts, a confusion now common, and in a great measure due to Ruskinian influence' (Stevenson, p. 405). But in 1854, Ruskin was right in his assumptions that such a method of reading was not a customary part of reviewing practice. To read *The awakening conscience*, to read the whole exhibition, not just as contemporary critics reported it. but as contemporary visitors might have understood it, means, in fact, placing it back in what we can recover of the context of 'reading' paintings at the time of the 1854 Academy exhibition. To do this involves using art history not as a means of celebrating an individual work, but of understanding the cultural complexity of a specific moment.

Note

I would like to thank all those who have discussed this paper with me, particularly John House, Marcia Pointon and Nigel Smith, for their invaluable help and encouragement.

4

Pre-Raphaelitism and Post-Raphaelitism: the articulation of fantasy and the problem of pictorial space
Paul Barlow

This chapter will principally comprise a detailed interpretation of Holman Hunt's early painting *The eve of St Agnes* (**10**). It will be argued that compositional features hitherto unconsidered in accounts of the work were significantly related to specific debates concerning the nature of pictorial space, which were central to the controversy which surrounded Pre-Raphaelitism in the 1850s. The peculiarities of Pre-Raphaelite work, its elaboration of surface, medievalism, concern with 'interrupted' human relationships, have been discussed in various ways but have never been accounted for as part of a response to a specific construction of pictorial space in the works of what Ruskin called 'the old school' of anecdotal historical/genre painters.[1] It will be argued that, far from being a pointlessly abstract form of explanation, these considerations are crucial for any account which claims to locate the pictorial procedures of the Pre-Raphaelites in the cultural situation from which they emerged. In Hunt's case the rejection of the particular use of pictorial space characteristic of 'the old school' was central to his project to reconstruct the pictorial conditions for an art which possessed ethical import, conditions which had been increasingly difficult to sustain since the decline of the Reynoldsian concept of History Painting in the Grand Manner. I shall start, therefore, from an implied question: What, in such a situation, would the pictorial structure of a painting which involved an ethical imperative involve?

In order to consider this question I shall discuss a pair of paintings exhibited at the British Institution in 1857 by Henry O'Neil, a virulent opponent of the Pre-Raphaelites.[2] These were exhibited under the title *The two extremes: the Prae-Raphaelite and the Post-Raphaelite*.[3] *The two extremes*

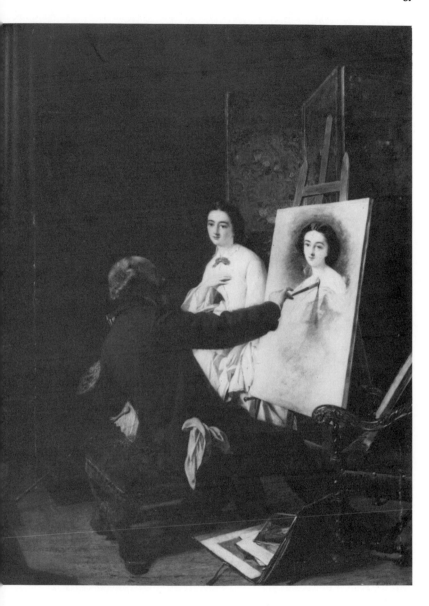

9 W. N. O'Neil, *Self-portrait (Painting con amore)*

embodies O'Neil's criticisms of the Pre-Raphaelites in pictorial form. The first 'extreme', *The Prae-Raphaelite*, depicted, according to the *Illustrated London news*:

a conceited looking young artist . . . painting with infinite labour, as may be seen from the minute specks of colour on his palette, in the style which he imagines was that anterior to the time of Raphael. He has two red-haired models posed, the one appealing to the other. These he is painting from in the most formal, hard, manner possible, and giving them the sourest of expressions; and we read in 'black letter' on the frame that the subject is to be 'Love and Duty'. The artist sits on his stool as if doing penance, with his long hair combed down with ascetic straightness. He wears a medieval mantle and the back of his studio is covered with a monster fresco.

The companion painting, *The Post-Raphaelite*, showed an artist who, by contrast, was:

working with the free abandonment of manner which, except when restrained by a theory, follows that mastery of the technical parts of the art which the more modern masters have helped succeeding artists to acquire. Mr. Palette is here dashing away at the portrait of a charming dark-haired girl, and as he sways backward and inclines his head on one side, you cannot help sympathising with the evident gusto with which he is giving that bold, yet light handed, stroke of the brush. (*Illustrated London news*, 30, 1857, p. 158)

Elsewhere the 'Post-Raphaelite' artist was described as 'a full whiskered neat man, leaning back at his easel and sweeping in a colour with his bent and pliant brush' (the *Athenaeum*, 14 Feb. 1857, p. 217).

Despite the fact that the original versions of both these paintings are unlocated, the descriptions of *The Post-Raphaelite* suggest that it corresponds precisely to a self-portrait painted by O'Neil in 1859 on commission for Patrick Allan-Fraser, a wealthy Scot who dabbled in the arts (Faberman, p. 224) (9). In a letter to Allan-Fraser dated 29 December 1859, O'Neil entitled the work *Painting con amore*.[4] O'Neil depicts himself 'full whiskered', leaning back from his easel, his head tilted. His brush is 'bent' against a canvas and his model is, as in the description, dark-haired.

If *Painting con amore* is a copy of *The Post-Raphaelite*, as it appears to be, then it can be read as a critique of the situation displayed in *The Prae-Raphaelite*. In the latter, we are told, an artist is working on a painting entitled *Love and duty*. This is presumably a reference to the series of works by Millais, initiated with *A Huguenot* . . . in 1852, though similar themes were explored by Holman Hunt in *Claudio and Isabella* (1850–53) and *Valentine rescuing Sylvia from Proteus* (1850–51).[5] In both Millais's and Hunt's paintings the fulfilment of desire is interrupted as a result of the ideological conflicts which constitute duty; the Huguenot leaves his fiancée and sets out to certain death, Proteus's designs on Sylvia are defeated, and in *Measure for measure* Isabella's chastity will remain intact. In each case the episodes depicted are those of maximum tension between the demands of 'love' and of 'duty', which are poised in perpetual antagonism. Though the lovers aspire to possess each other they are doomed to remain forever thwarted by the spectre of duty. This condition of permanently frozen desire is, it would seem likely, that in which the protagonists of *Love and duty* also found themselves, posed awkwardly, appealing one to the other.

Painting con amore delineates a very different situation. It concerns access to the body of the loved one. The 'ascetic' Prae-Raphaelite was locked in the 'infinite labour' of the elaboration of the surface of his painting; the 'Post-Raphaelite', O'Neil, engages in the task of stripping away the covering surface. The portrait of the young woman at which O'Neil is working is juxtaposed with the model herself, so that the angle at which the model is viewed is identical to the pose of the figure on the canvas. The canvas on which the portrait is painted is depicted at an angle to the surface of the painting as a whole, but the image within it retains its coherence for the viewer, seeming thereby to float free of support. Thus the power to dissolve surface is construed as a feature of the Post-Raphaelitism of the painter. Against this may be set the self-denying duty which the Prae-Raphaelite masochistically imposes upon himself infinitely to elaborate surface, never achieving the satisfaction of desire implied by its penetration. For such penetration of surface is implicitly equated with notional access to the body of the subject.

Let me elaborate. In the process of painting the model O'Neil is also undressing her. The model herself is primarily attired in a tight white dress. Her painted counterpart is naked above the breast, her only visible clothing a thin whisp of pink cloth loosely held over her breasts by her right hand. O'Neil's brush not only penetrates the surface of the canvas, it also, in effect, paints out the woman's clothing, revealing her body to the gaze of the artist and the viewer. This is, indeed, painting 'con amore'. In terms of the title of the Prae-Raphaelite painting, O'Neil achieves the 'love' which the Pre-Raphaelite himself is denied in his perpetual thrall to duty.

The two extremes illustrates the relationship and differences between the Pre-Raphaelite construction of the function of pictorial space in relation to narrative and that of an alternative, jokingly termed 'Post-Raphaelitism', which proposes the myth of dissolution of the surface, notional access to the body within representation, and the fantasy of incorporation into pictorial space. This was a crucial difference between the work of 'the old school' and that of the Pre-Raphaelites. The same pictorial structures can be found in the works of many other artists of O'Neil's circle, particularly those who formed the group known as 'The Clique'.[6] These structures derive from the connection between the tradition of anecdotal genre painting initiated by Wilkie and the specific features of the illustrations to the so-called Keepsake annuals, popular albums of poetry, short stories and engravings familiar in the 1840s. O'Neil, like many other contemporary artists, had begun his career providing illustrations to such volumes.[7] The portrait he paints in The Post-Raphaelite is a typical Keepsake image, an isolated female figure gazing wistfully into nowhere. The Keepsake promoted a particular form of relationship between viewer and image in which the construction of fantastic narratives concerning the figures in accompanying engravings were encouraged.

This tendency to treat paintings in terms of their capacity to produce the conditions for the construction of fantasies concerning the individuals represented in them, rather than as pictorial constructs, saturates the art criticism of the period in which the Pre-Raphaelite Brotherhood was formed.[8] It is against this that the peculiarly Pre-Raphaelite constitution of pictorial space can be characterised. An analysis of Holman Hunt's The eve of St Agnes provides the opportunity for an understanding of this process. It was The eve of St Agnes (**10**), exhibited at the Royal Academy in 1848, that brought the three founders of the Brotherhood together as a group. It is appropriate, therefore, to consider its departure from the characterisation of pictorial space embodied by the artists who, like O'Neil, developed from the Keepsake tradition their own 'Post-Raphaelite' concern with the notional penetration of the surface of the image and the initiation of fantasised involvement with its represented world.

Hunt's painting illustrates a stanza from Keats's poem The eve of St Agnes in which the escape of the lovers Madeline and Porphyro from the house of Madeline's hostile family is described:

> They glide, like phantoms, into the wide hall;
> Like phantoms, to the iron porch, they glide;
> Where lay the Porter, in uneasy sprawl,
> With a huge empty flagon by his side:
> The wakeful bloodhound rose, and shook his hide,
> But his sagacious eye an inmate owns:
> By one, and one, the bolts full easy slide; –
> The chains lie silent on the footworn stones; –
> The key turns, and the door upon its hinges groans (stanza 41)

The lovers are depicted at the right of the composition, about to open the door but poised uncertainly as the 'wakeful bloodhound' seems about to raise the alarm. The drunken revellers, Porphyro's enemies, are visible in a room at the left while the porter sprawls in a complex foreshortened pose in the centre.

The moment depicted is the conclusion of a narrative of voyeuristic desire which consistently skirts the borders of pornography, consequently endangering the poem's status as public, even elevated, discourse. Keats's techniques involve the enlistment of fantasy in a way which resembles the conventions of Keepsake literature and of O'Neil's 'Post-Raphaelitism'. But Keats's elicits the desire of the (male) reader for the body of Madeline while playing upon the fact that such desire can only be satisfied through the fantasy which the text produces as its 'poetic' values. The description of the fulfilment of desire thus becomes the point at which poetic language is most urgently required. Keats described the sexual union of the lovers in the famous simile:

Into her dream he melted, as the rose
Blendeth its odour with the violet, –
Solution sweet: (Stanza 36)

The dissolution into colour, odour and simile is also an act of fantasy, for Porphyro melts 'into her dream'. But the contrast with the cold, dead, monochrome world of wakefulness, on which Keats insists (as in the first and last verses), is crucial. The reader, like the sculptur'd dead ... Emprison'd in black, purgatorial rails' (Stanza 2), is excluded from the pleasures enjoyed by the lovers. The events occur in a vaguely medieval past, an alien 'romantic' environment in which desires are satisfied and fantasies formed into realities. But this is only for the lovers themselves. The reader is distanced temporarily and textually from the action. The inevitable loss involved for the reader when woken from the 'dream', the gap between reality and fantasy, is indicated by the sudden change of tense between the penultimate and the last stanza. After the 'groans' of the door-hinge, the poem shifts suddenly into the past tense:

And they are gone: ay, ages long ago
These lovers fled away into the storm. (Stanza 42)

The text then concludes with a description of the lonely and ugly death of two elderly minor characters. The imaginary world of the poem has dissolved at the very moment the lovers enter the cold, harsh reality of the storm outside and as the reader is reminded of the gulf between that moment and the other 'present', the moment of reading.

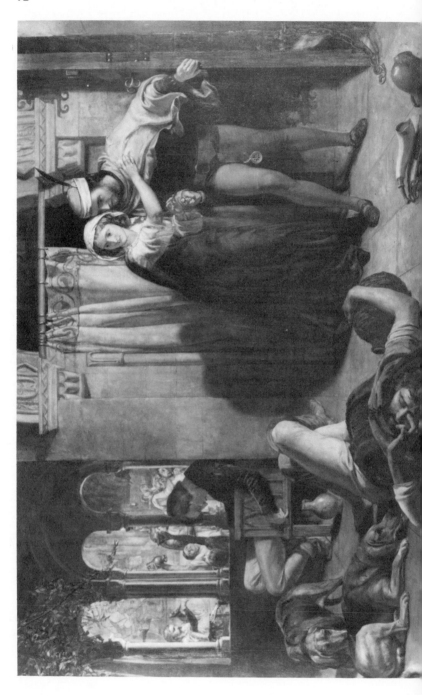

This, then, is the crucial point in the text which provides the subject of Hunt's painting. In terms of the narrative it is the moment of maximum tension. The groaning of the hinges, the waking of the porter, the howling of the dog, all could bring down on the lovers' heads the wrath of the 'bloated wassailers' in the nearby room. The image is poised in perpetual tension, Porphyro preparing to unsheath his sword for violent action but being restrained by Madeline. The painting is thus held between an explosion into dramatic activity and the conclusion of its narrative outside its own space, as the lovers move from art out into the real, natural, world on the other side of the door/frame. The door opens out into a 'nature' beyond the space of the image, a reality as inaccessible to the painting as the actual intimacy of the lovers was to the reader of the poem. It proposes, therefore, the absence of nature as a necessary condition of art, the reverse of the 'Post-Raphaelite' aesthetic of O'Neil. The painting, like the poem, is caught in the space between the fantasy of real sexual satisfaction in an 'other' time and the reality that such satisfaction is only the imagined product of an artificial construct, operating through the pictorial language of the image itself. If the poetic diction of Keats's text, involving the use of metaphor and simile, was the location of the articulation of fantasy, in the painting this role is taken by the terms of the construction of the image itself, a narrative of colour, line and space.

The sexuality of Hunt's lovers is suggested metaphorically through their clothing. An unmistakably phallic leather belt dangles between Porphyro's legs. Madeline's body, in contrast, is enveloped in a long purple dress surrounded by an amorphous shadow. In this case the purple of Madeline's dress corresponds to the dissolution of consciousness in Keats's simile of the rose and the violet. But the differences between the ways in which Porphyro's sexuality is represented, by pictorial metaphor, and the equation of Madeline's body with a mass of colour spread across the surface of the image, is that between the desiring and the desired. The significance of this, however, only becomes evident once the figure of the porter is considered.

The juxtaposition of the porter with the lovers signals the relationship between the problems of reality and fantasy, which Hunt has taken from Keats's poem, and his analysis of the status of pictorial space. Like the lovers, the porter has indulged in sensuous pleasure, in this case the consumption of alcohol. His 'uneasy sprawl' takes the form of an extremely foreshortened view of his body, which is seen leaning almost beyond the field of the image into our own space. The upraised left hand and the head against which it leans appear to tip over the edge of the

10 W. Holman Hunt, The eve of St. Agnes

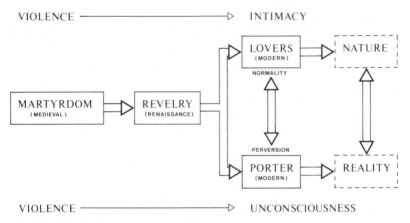

Diagram of *The eve of St Agnes*

notional space. In fact the foreshortening itself seems 'uneasy', producing the sense that the body is crushed up against the surface of the image.
This is due to the somewhat confused perspectival construction. The
space follows a roughly accurate single point perspectival scheme but the
cues to recession tend to be obscured. Most corners are hidden by
objects or shadows. Even the base of the pillar beneath which the porter
is seen is scarcely differentiated from the stone flags of the hallway, which
are painted in an identical grey–brown. Most of the forms are read across
the space rather than in depth and consequently have a flat, two-dimensional, appearance. Furthermore, the composition itself recedes in a
series of diminishing rectangles rather than in properly articulated depth.

The curiously distorted pose of the porter is the counterpart to Keats's
change of tense, the point which establishes the gulf between the world
of the poem and of its reader. In Hunt's painting, the lovers, as stated
above, are about to leave the space of the image to enter the visually
excluded realm of nature, represented by the undifferentiated blur of
green at the extreme right. But the porter seems also to be about to leave
the space of the painting; his head and hand apparently invade the real
space outside it. There is, thus, a double reference to the borders of the
imaginary realm of the image. In both cases these involve figures associated with sensuous satisfaction, unconsciousness and dreams. The
porter, of course, is a conventional figure of brute sensual indulgence,
familiar from Dutch genre painting. But he also represents a possible
relationships of the viewer to the space of the image. Keat's last stanza
established the distance between the fantasy of the narrative and the

inevitable loss of the body which poetic language cannot fully restore, the 'cold' world outside. Hunt's painting contrasts the 'real' satisfaction of the lovers in the fantasy space of the image with the sleeping body of the porter who is in an oddly distorted, perverse, relationship to the space and is unconscious of the action. In these respects he is an alien figure in the image, and thus functions in a rhetorically analogous way to Keats's change of tense, as a *memento mori*, or at least as the ineradicable difference between the real space outside the image and the construction of fantasy narratives. The gesture of the porter's left hand, resting against his head, is a traditional sign of profound thought. It closely resembles, for example, the pose of St John in Raphael's *Transfiguration*, as he is overwhelmed by the spiritual forms of Christ, Moses and Elijah who float above him. The closed eyes and thoughtful gesture of the porter, combined with his perverse relationship with the space of the image, imply a further analogy with the viewer of the painting. In this the porter stands analogically for the process of fantasising the world of the image in which the viewer engages. The painting may, in this sense, be thought of as the dream of the porter.

At this point the crucial differences between Hunt's methods and O'Neil's 'Post-Raphaelitism' are becoming evident. If the porter stands in for the viewer, he does so in a way which stresses the contradictions involved in the mythic dissolution of pictorial surface which O'Neil produces. While the subject of the painting concerns fantasies of access to the body of Madeline (just as numerous works by O'Neil and his circle, derived from the conventions of Keepsake imagery, had constructed similar imaginary feminine presences),[9] the sprawling porter implicitly asserts the potential deceptions of fantasy. If O'Neil's aesthetic involved the denial of visual artifice, Hunt's technique reasserts it, though from within the very pictorial language which had allowed its notional suppression. The porter in this way carries the ethical force of the painting, which is one reason why the lovers gaze towards him, having themselves awoken from their fantasies as they approach the real, cold world outside the image. Hunt thus stresses the borders of artifice as the point at which the contradictions between fantasy and reality are negotiated.

The figures at the edge of the pictorial space are in fact the final episodes of a systematic analysis of stages from artifice into reality. This starts with the tapestry or mural depicting a violent event, probably a martyrdom. This is the furthest visible point from the notional location of the painting's surface. This part of the image is very crudely painted.

The lines defining the figures are left visible, colour is reduced to thinly applied marks of blue and red from beneath which the ground is clearly visible. Spacial recession, therefore, is made to correspond to the increasing visibility of the means of pictorial representation.

In front of the tapestry various figures can be seen drinking and dancing. The pictorial origins of this scene would seem to be the bacchanal paintings of Titian and Poussin. Though not explicitly violent, this scene is certainly energetic. It is also potentially violent because these are the lovers' enemies, whose presence necessitates their stealth. These figures are more subtly delineated than those in the tapestry but their intention is limited by the rhetorical patterns of gesture and expression which their pictorial sources convey.

A relationship is evident between degrees of violence and the development of the means of representation. Added to this is the implication of chronological progress from medieval conventions in the tapestry to those of the Renaissance in the scene in front of it. Just as the latter scene encompasses the former, so the foreground scene contains them both. But at this point the progress splits into the two channels through which the image probes its margins. Both the porter and the lovers are painted in full detail. The couple are combined in a relationship which is not reducible to the rhetoric of gesture used for the revellers. The particular event depicted is an act of restraint from violence, where dramatic gesture is being suppressed. In terms of the move from depth to surface and from artifice to nature this is the limit of representation, displaying 'that mastery of the technical parts of the art which the more modern masters have helped succeeding artists to acquire' (on O'Neil's The two extremes, Illustrated London news, 30, 1857, p. 158). But whereas O'Neil simply presents himself as possessing that 'mastery', enabling him to cross the boundary between image and reality, Hunt incorporates it into his analysis of the necessary conflicts between the two. Rhetoric, the dramatics of gesture as a mode of pictorial articulation, a mode which characterises the depiction of the revellers, is in the process of suppression. But its complete suppression, which would be the end of artifice, can only occur outside the image in real space. If the lovers complete the progress from artifice to nature across the image from left to right, the porter completes it from within to without. His twisted, foreshortened body is the antithesis of the flat, crudely marked tapestry. His unconscious passivity is the opposite of its violent action. His is also a limiting case, in this instance of the extent of bodily intrusion into space, of the defiance of surface.

The split between the porter and lovers at this, the final stage within the image, of the progres from artifice to reality is, therefore, a means to maintain the internal coherence of the image. For O'Neil and his circle the dissolution of surface involves the combination of the fantasising viewer with the object of fantasy in a notional penetration of artifice. Here the fantasising viewer is also the unconscious porter. The object of the fantasy is the union of the lovers or, in O'Neil's terms, the 'undressing' of Madeline and the equation of the viewer with Porphyro. Such a process is implied but subverted. The penetration never occurs, only a schism which reflects the ultimately irresolvable difference between real presence and construed artifact. *The eve of St Agnes* thus functions as a critique of the pictorial production of fantasy. It undermines at its conclusion the progressive movement from artifice to reality. It turns back on itself once it reaches the border between the two. This is Hunt's confrontation with the problem of style from within a pictorial regime which presupposes a norm of notional stylelessness. It is through these mechanisms that pictorial morality is established, a concern which was to dominate Hunt's thinking about art throughout his career. The irresolvable nature of the antagonisms which the encroachment of the image on to reality produces exposes the paradoxes which the myth of stylelessness suppresses. In *The eve of St Agnes* this remains underdeveloped, but in later works like *The awakening conscience* and *Claudio and Isabella* these issues are more explicitly related to the painting's subject. In both these cases the space of the image is equated with imprisonment, literally in the latter work, metaphorically in the former.

These concerns were not unique to Hunt. Millais and Rossetti, in different ways, addressed the problem of style in a way which equally undermines the aesthetic so staunchly defined by O'Neil in *Painting con amore* (**9**). Rossetti's paintings of single female figures, for example, are in the same relationship to Keepsake imagery of the kind O'Neil depicts himself painting, as *The eve of St Agnes* (**10**) is to any of that artist's more ambitious works. This is perhaps clearest in *The blessed Damozel* (**11**) which illustrates Rossetti's own poem of the same name. In the poem the very blessedness of the Damozel imprisons her within a space which offers no outlet for sensuality. The poet signals the sexual attractions and desires of the Damozel which are condemned to remain forever unfulfilled in the 'vast waste calm' of heaven. The lines concerning her attempts to reach beyond this space instance Rossetti's insistence on corporeality with a context of unwanted spiritual calm:

. . . her bosom's pressure must have made,
The bar she leaned on warm (Stanza 8).

Rossetti's use of poetic language as a sign of other-worldliness parallels
Keats's method of associating the 'other' world of the poem, where
fantasies are articulated, with the poetic function and reach of metaphor.
The conventional iconography of spiritual revelation, paraded by Rossetti in the opening stanzas, contradicts the narrative of unsatisfied desire.
Thus instead of establishing a temporal gulf between reader and narrative, as Keats does in The eve of St Agnes, Rossetti inserts the desired and
desiring figure of the Damozel in a space accessible only in terms of
poetic convention.

The device used in the poem has obvious similarities with the way in
which the painting, The blessed Damozel (11), represents the spiritual realm.
She is seen leaning over the gold bar which runs across the centre of the
painting. She holds the three lilies and stars encircle her head. Angelic
and seraphic figures surround her. The figure of the Damozel's absent
lover, who is still on earth, is placed in a separate panel. The spiritual
realm is defined as such, therefore, by the adoption of highly conven-
tionalised imagery and shallow, perspectival space associated with Quattrocento art. For O'Neil and his circle this was simply a nonsensical
archaism. As he wrote in Two thousand years hence, Pre-Raphaelite paintings
have 'so great an affinity to the production of the artists of medieval times
that, but for the date being conspicuously painted on them, it would be
impossible to believe that they were produced at the period I treat of'
(p. 222). But in The blessed Damozel the existence of a living woman with
earthly concerns is imagined behind the conventional imagery. Those
conventions are themselves justified as a depiction of the non-natural
realm of the spirit from which the Damozel is then understood to wish to
escape. This is an approach to Quattrocento conventions which implies
the same assumptions as Keepsake imagery, the need to supersede
artifice. Like the woman in The awakening conscience (5), the Damozel is
caught in artifice, the display of which suppresses the fantasy of incorporation into the space of the image which 'Post-Raphaelitism' promotes.
The ethical import of Hunt's work is, of course, absent from Rossetti's,
which implies, in fact, that the very conditions of purity towards which
the woman in The awakening conscience aspires, are themselves a form of
imprisonment. But this very difference illustrates the structured identity
of these different works when viewed in relation to the 'Post-Raphaelite'
aesthetic.

11 D. G. Rossetti, The blessed Damozel

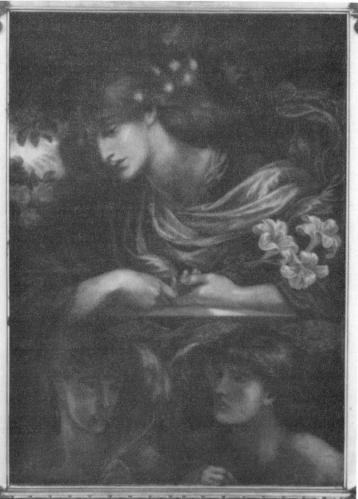

THE BLESSED DAMOZEL

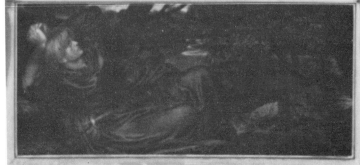

O'Neil's *The two extremes* was a response to Pre-Raphaelitism by an artist whose own pictorial practices were already well established. It is an unusually clear instance of the relationship of those features which constitute Pre-Raphaelitism to an aesthetic which it presupposes while attempting to reject it. It is only by comparing the aesthetic logic of Pre-Raphaelitism with the structures of the art that O'Neil terms 'Post-Raphaelite' that specifically historical accounts of the pictorial challenge offered by such works can avoid reductionism on the one hand and the myth of the avant garde on the other. O'Neil's own work, together with that of artists closely associated with him, such as E. M. Ward, Alfred Elmore and John Phillip, involves the exploration of the implications of the equation of reality with an achieved 'modernity', a norm of pictorial representation which allows for the mythic suppression of surface. This equation of nature/reality with an achieved (Post-Raphaelite) norm is what Pre-Raphaelitism sets out to subvert. In this respect Ruskinian detail and medievalising artifice are equally means of subverting the rationale of the natural norm. For Ruskin, nature inevitably supersedes the grasp of any artist and can therefore never form the basis of a teachable aesthetic norm.[10] The relationship between the ultimately incomprehensible natural world and the activity of the artist is never definitively established. Consequently it is perpetually renegotiable. Thus the very excess implied by the demand that the artist should rely absolutely on nature enables Ruskin to reinvent a language of style. If the paradox of 'Post-Raphaelitism' was that the myth of stylelessness depended upon an implied concensus in matters of style, then Ruskin's demands are radical to the extent that they undermine the very idea of such a consensus.

Ruskin's ideas may be said to concern the inevitable failure of a norm of representation to comprehend that which, by definition, lies beyond it: Nature. Even an early work of Hunt's like *The eve of St Agnes*, painted when he was only slightly acquainted with Ruskin's writings, is largely consistent with such a theory. The later works indicate the extent to which this idea of the failure of representation fitted the demands of Hunt's characteristically proscriptive ethical narratives. But neither Ruskin's nor Hunt's attempts to deal with the problems of the aesthetic presented by O'Neil as the norm from which the Pre-Raphaelites have deviated can be properly understood until the aesthetic itself has been thoroughly investigated.

Pre-Raphaelitism has been for so long isolated from supposedly 'conventional' Victorian painting that the specific pictorial logic of its deviation from the predominant form of contemporary narrative painting has been obscured. The sterility of accounts which interpret contemporary attacks on Pre-Raphaelitism as examples of knee-jerk conservatism have been rightly condemned. It has been suggested that such analyses evade proper consideration of the discursive constructs from which the attacks derive and thereby reproduce uncritically the myth of the avant garde. Nevertheless, by ignoring the relationship between the pictorial logic of Pre-Raphaelitism and the structures of the art which is here termed Post-Raphaelitism, such accounts risk a reductionism which reproduces the myth that most Victorian painting is essentially aesthetically neutral, or 'merely illustrative'. The meanings of both Pre-Raphaelite and anti-Pre-Raphaelite painting involve concerns about the extent and limits of representational space, concerns which define the range of those meanings. The specific nature and extent of these differences would justify further examination. This chapter has concentrated on identifying this defining characteristic of Pre-Raphaelitism, its rejection of a representational norm which implicitly claims to suppress artifice. Such an analysis is vital if much is not to remain obscure or misrepresented when accounts of the origin of the movement are given.

Notes

1 Ruskin uses this term in his *Academy notes* when attacking works by E. M. Ward and Alfred Elmore. Cf. Ruskin, 14, pp. 52, 56.
2 He attacked them in a number of his writings, notably in his eccentric fantasy *Two thousand years hence* in which an archaeologist of the year 3867 uncovers works by painters whose apparent intention was to 'produce the outward materialism rather than the spirit of nature; – to paint every object in the minutest detail, as it was seen and not as it was felt' (O'Neil, p. 223).
3 Neither work has been located and they are known only from contemporary descriptions.
4 MS., Patrick Allan-Fraser Trust, Hospitalfield House, Arbroath.
5 *A Huguenot, on St. Bartholomew's day, refusing to shield himself from danger by wearing the Roman Catholic badge*, Makins collection; *Claudio and Isabella*, Tate Gallery; *Valentine rescuing Sylvia from Proteus*, Birmingham Museum and Art gallery, all reproduced in *The Pre-Raphaelites*.
6 'The Clique' was a sketching society comprising Richard Dadd, Henry O'Neil, W. P. Frith, E. M. Ward, Alfred Elmore, Augustus Egg and John Phillip. They met regularly at Dadd's lodgings for a short period at the end of the 1830s. After Dadd's departure for the Middle East they ceased to meet regularly but remained friends. They all, however, employed in their works devices similar to those found in O'Neil's *The Post-Raphaelite*.
7 Keepsake engravings were generally portraits of young women with faraway expressions. They were much criticised by the Pre-Raphaelites, among others, for alleged banality or insipidity. O'Neil contributed both verses and images to the Keepsake for 1855. He also supplied material to other productions in the Keepsake manner, as did most other members of the Clique.

8 Reviewers of exhibitions writing in periodicals and newspapers during the 1830s and
   1840s tended to adopt standards of judgement involving the idea that 'healthy' art should
   not display any of the terms of its construction, or at any rate, that it was not the province
   of the critic to draw attention to such matters, but rather to judge the effect which the
   artist had conveyed. Wilkie, in his notes on the art of painting (published in Cunningham's The life of David Wilkie, London, 1843), even declared that 'democratic' painting
   necessarily involved the concealment of the 'tricks' of composition, colour and so on, so
   that the spectator could experience the picture as a 'dream' and be 'transported' into the
   world it depicts (Cunningham, 3, p. 151).
9 E.g. Ward's La toilette des morts (1863, private collection), Frith's The sleepy model (1853, Royal
   Academy), Elmore's The invention of the combing machine (1862, Cartwright Hall, Bradford)
   and Phillip's numerous images of Spanish women.
10 This is the theoretical basis of Ruskin's defence of Turner. Cf. Ruskin, 3, passim.

5

The elusive depth of field: stereoscopy and the Pre-Raphaelites
Lindsay Smith

The invention of photography represents a crisis point in the relationship of the spectator to phenomena and creates singular hermeneutical problems. Photography is inseparable from a complex nineteenth-century discourse of optics. This discourse manifests itself in distinctive optical instruments as direct precursors of and elaborate supplements to the camera. However, all too frequently in art historical debates photography is wrenched from its intertextual origins and the nature and extent of the upheaval it caused are strategically overlooked. On its emergence in the late 1840s, Pre-Raphaelitism was invariably defined in relationship to this new, disruptive practice of photography. However, attempts to pinpoint the influence of photography on Pre-Raphaelite painting generally aspire to construe photography as a homogeneous discourse, smoothing over its internal contradictions, forgetful of its controversial political and theoretical ramifications.[1] I shall discuss Pre-Raphaelitism in relation to a culturally specific Victorian optical practice, that of stereoscopy.[2]

In the case of the Pre-Raphaelites a re-staging of the workings of perceptual aberration is crucial to textual as well as visual concerns. Both photography and Pre-Raphaelitism explore a common concern for perceptual aberration, or optical trickery, as articulated by the depth of field. It is the stereoscopic photograph that most dramatically mobilises the phenomenon of depth of field and calls attention to the eyes' potential for manipulation. Furthermore, stereoscopy constitutes a productive model/metaphor for the types of visual perplexity which certain Pre-Raphaelite paintings arouse. As quite literally a re-statement of illusionism, by way of its restoration of the sovereignty of two eyes over one, stereoscopy by contrast to 'monoscopy' foregrounds the process by which depth of field is newly fashioned. It re-inscribes the illusionism of depth.

I do not claim that generally speaking Pre-Raphaelite paintings have or suggest stereoscopic counterparts/corollaries. I have no desire to mediate the one discourse through the other. But rather I wish to argue that both Pre-Raphaelitism and the newly developing practice of stereoscopic photography re-problematise depth of field and thereby engage a shared cultural and political debate.

By concentrating upon Millais's The woodman's daughter (12), which has been considered from the outset a problematic painting, and upon Coventry Patmore's poem of the same title on which the painting was based, I will show how specific intertextual concerns have been elided by criticism. Moreover, I will argue that the process of mythologising the Pre-Raphaelite Brotherhood has been achieved only at the expense of dislocating it from a culturally and historically complex optical discourse which, during the 1840s and 1850s, was manifesting itself in new photographic instruments and practices. The photograph is a radical culmination of a long-standing optical discourse which has been repeatedly de-historicised. Not only have the precursors of photography been eclipsed, but fashionable crazes like that of the stereoscope have been removed from intertextual debate. One reads erroneous accounts of early photography that construct it in an unproblematically threatening relationship to painting by way of its so-called superior realism. However, from its inception photography forges a complex reciprocal interchange with painting. In other words, there occurs during this period an inevitable identification of Pre-Raphaelitism and photography, but the political and culturally specific nature of this identification remains a difficult subject for art criticism.[3]

This is not to say that critics do not seek analogues for photography in Pre-Raphaelite painting. On the contrary, it is curious the way in which a generalised version of photographic practice becomes an all too simple explanation of the perplexing radical optical fidelity of the Pre-Raphaelites. Critics align conditions of photographic exactitude with microscopic detail in discussion of Pre-Raphaelite technique, and contemporary reviewers criticise, by implication, Pre-Raphaelitism's preoccupation with that which was previously invisible.[4] However, such references to microscopic clarity elide precisely those culturally specific relationships of Pre-Raphaelitism with innovative optical devices, those relationships which characterise a singular crisis point in visual perception and representation. In short, critics, ironically, have sought analogues in the wrong instruments, in the microscope and the camera.

It is significant that the debt/similarity of Pre-Raphaelite painting to photographic exactitude has become almost a household word while what has been forgotten in the forging of this correspondence is not only the disruption in visual experience caused by photography but also the fact that it was an unprecedented term of reference, an innovative analogy. Prior to J. N. Niépce's invention, painting's potentiality for verisimilitude had other determinants. Indeed the first photograph radically altered the trompe l'oeil of painting.[5] At this historical juncture photography provides a new criterion by which we may read painting. This point alone renders photography pertinent to the social/cultural positioning of the Pre-Raphaelites.

Both Pre-Raphaelitism and stereoscopy articulate a newly arousing depth of field. Indeed the stereoscopic image calls attention to itself as mediated in a manner different from any previous optical instrument. The stereoscope harbours within itself the shift from monoscopy which empowers a different relationship of beholder to the percept. Or, more emphatically, the stereograph subverts the monopoly of 'monoscopy' or monocular vision in the field of optical mediation, and thereby re-establishes the sovereignty of the two eyes. We may witness the struggle for such sovereignty within Millais's painting.

The shift from monocular to stereoscopic vision may be located in a change from a privileged Romantic spectator who is usually an artist to a Victorian optically-educated and 'ordinary' spectator.[6] A greater democratic relationship to the visual field is implied such that Ruskin, for example, asserts that a labour of vision elicits recognition of the sovereignty of 'the desire of the eyes'.[7] Ruskin encourages his young female drawing students to take to nature their pocket magnifying glasses, but he denounces the popular Romantic instrument, the Claude-glass, precisely because it presents an indirect mediation.[8] The spectator has to turn her back on the landscape in order to witness the image in the mirror. Not only does the Claude-glass give a false representation, since it condenses the whole scene, but it also performs a lateral inversion of it. It is important to note that this instrument does not privilege depth of field.

Ruskin regarded the Claude-glass as 'one of the most pestilent inventions for falsifying nature and degrading art which ever was put into an artist's hand'.[9] In the manner of the camera obscura and the camera lucida, an optical instrument that could be attached to the eyepiece of a microscope to enable the containment and tracing of an image, the Claude-glass is characterised by the fact that the scene is viewed within a frame. The frame of the instrument formulates the scene. By contrast, the stereoscope does not require the subject's consciousness of the frame. Indeed, sight of the binocular frames prohibits the possibility of stereoscopic effect. The stereoscope is, in addition, distinguished from standard monoscopic instruments by its ability, to some extent, to annihilate itself as medium. It seemingly annuls itself because its effect inverts its cause or origin; two photographs seen with two eyes give one image. The stereoscope does not attempt to elucidate the unseen or to transcend the power of the eye in the manner of the telescope or the microscope. Ruskin denounces the latter because it enables the eye to transgress its so-called natural bounds and the former because he believes it performs a different but equally transgressive gesture – it brings into focus other worlds whose cratered surfaces bear little relation to the earth's.[10] By contrast, Ruskin permits magnifying glasses, for they merely compensate for minor defects in the eye. They do not render visible the previously invisible, and they may be used with two eyes. Thus the rationale for this particular Ruskinian legitimation derives from the belief that the ultimate optical transgression is, so to speak, to disrupt invisibility.

Ruskin's defence of the Pre-Raphaelites derives in part from his recognition of the contradictory aspects of reviews which identified 'microscopic' clarity when the Pre-Raphaelites were intent upon transcribing whole scenes as viewed by the two eyes stereoscopically. As Ruskin writes in chapter four of *Modern painters*, 1, 'the eye like any other lens, must have its focus altered, in order to convey a distinct image of objects at different distances'. In a footnote to this account he explains shifting focus as a requisite for natural perception which is stereoscopic. The principle of binocular vision which forms the basis of stereoscopic photography is produced by the mental fusion of the slightly dissimilar images seen by the two eyes into one image giving the effect of solidity. Euclid noted the distinction of the two images as early as 280 BC. But it was not until 1832 that Sir Charles Wheatstone invented the first instrument by which the stereoscopic effect could be observed, combining two drawings from the slightly different viewpoints of the eyes. In the latter part of that year he had stereoscopes of two types (one with reflecting mirrors, the other with refracting prisms) made for him by the London opticians Murray and Heath. A brief notice of his observations appeared in Herbert Mayo's *Outlines of human physiology* in 1837. But because he was occupied during the next five years with the electric telegraph, Wheatstone put to one side his paper on stereoscopy.[11]

It was in fact David Brewster's refracting or lenticular stereoscope, described to the Royal Society of Edinburgh in 1849, that established public interest and transformed the instrument from a scientific tool for studying the physiology of vision to an enormously popular source of entertainment. However, Brewster had initially to publicise his instrument in France, and it was only after the French optician Jules Duboscq constructed a number of stereoscopes for the Great Exhibition of 1851 (including an elaborate instrument for Queen Victoria) that English opticians began to manufacture stereoscopes. Nearly a quarter of a million were sold in London and Paris within three months. In 1854 George Swan Nottage founded the London Stereoscopic Company for the manufacture and sale of lenticular stereoscopes and binocular pictures, and by 1858 the company advertised a stock of 100,000 different photographs and had staff acquiring views in the Middle East and America. The stereograph harnesses otherwise unknown views. Antoine Claudet, the leading daguerreotypist, noted that

it introduces us to scenes known only from the imperfect relations of travellers . . . by our fireside we have the advantage of examining them without being exposed to the fatigue, privation, and risks of the daring and enterprising artists who, for our gratification and instruction, have travelled lands and seas . . . ascended rocks and mountains with their heavy and cumbrous baggage.[12]

Thus the stereoscope became widely disseminated. In 1858 a lending library began in London which, for an annual subscription of one guinea, allowed the public to change their stereographs as often as they wished. In the same year The stereoscopic magazine was introduced, a periodical dedicated solely to the instrument, which came complete with binocular viewer.[13] According to Gernsheim, 'with increasing popularity, a lowering of tastes set in; the stereoscope became the poor man's picture gallery' (Gernsheim, p. 258). And his rather telling reasoning suggests that the instument fell into disrepute precisely because it was disseminated so easily. Moreover, its staging of narrative proved potentially uncontainable. It is not therefore surprising that it was replaced by 1862 as a craze by the carte-de-visite, in which staged narrative had been replaced by the self-portrait, nor that the first cartes were of the royal family and of those in aristocratic circles. Unlike the stereograph's staging of depth the carte substituted self for signature and shifted attention away from a mediating instrument.[14]

It is Brewster's account of the stereoscope, his rhetoric of its legitimacy, that interests me, in part because of its intertextual bias. The introductory paragraph of his book The stereoscope, its history, theory, and *construction* (1856), attempts to legitimate the instrument by stressing its opposition to monocular vision. It shows how the stereoscope could by definition divorce itself from Ruskin's vilification. The stereoscope, from the Greek for 'solid' and 'to see':

is an optical instrument of modern invention, for representing, in apparent relief and solidity, all natural objects and all groups as seen by each eye separately. In its most general form, the stereoscope is binocular . . . [It] therefore, cannot, like the telescope and microscope, be used by persons who have lost the use of one eye, and its remarkable effects be properly appreciated by those whose eyes are not equally good. . . . in monocular vision we learn from experience to estimate all distances, but particularly great ones, by various means, which are called the criteria of distance; but it is only with both eyes that we can estimate with anything like accuracy the distance of objects not far from us.[15]

Brewster's work forges for the discourse of optics new contextual relationships. The *Letters on natural magic addressed to Sir Walter Scott* (1832), which precedes his experiments in stereoscopy, performs an intertextual examination of optics which he claims is 'of all sciences . . . the most fertile in marvellous expedients'. Brewster uses Scott's name to authorise his discussion and he produces a history for optics, establishing his letters as part of developing discourse. In this text Brewster's account of the Brocken Spectre and the subsequent re-inscription of the narrative by Thomas De Quincey in *Suspiria de profundis* (1845), constitutes a culturally productive intermediary between aspects of Romantic monocular vision and Victorian stereoscopic vision.[16] It is a pivotal point in the disruption of the monocular monopoly. Brewster elucidates the Brocken Spectre along with other analoguous phenomena such as the *fata morgana* of the Straits of Messina and the spectre ships. The Brocken is the name of the loftiest of the Hartz Mountains, and Brewster writes that it has 'since the earliest periods of authentic history been the seat of the marvelous' (p. 199). The history of the Spectre resides in accounts of its elusive nature, and Brewster cites as 'one of the best accounts' that given by M. Haue 'who saw it on 23 May, 1797, after having been on the summit no less than thirty times' (p. 199). It appears as 'a human figure of a monstrous size' and it is projected from the observer's body on to 'dense vapour or thin fleecy clouds which have the effect of reflecting much light' (p. 221). The subject's body is the medium that produces the elusive Brocken Spectre. Since the Spectre is literally a projection of the subject's body, Brewster stresses the uncanny status of the double.

The method of De Quincey's re-writing of Brewster foregrounds the double and the transformation in optical illusionism/mediation. The metaphorical appropriation of the spectre serves as a figure for and is figured by 'the dark interpreter'. However, the spectre performs other functions. In one sense, De Quincey is concerned with its history, together with that of the 'sorcerer's flower', which once 'glorified the worship of fear' and remains a reminder of the 'gloomy realities of Paganism'. In another sense, De Quincey harnesses the spectre primarily as a double for the dark interpreter whose reflex action and alien nature it shares. Moreover, the spectre and the dark interpreter are both able to 'dissemble' their real origins, for as De Quincey writes of the dark interpreter, 'I do not always know him in these cases as my own parhelion.' The use here of the term 'parhelion', literally a bright spot near the sun, a 'mock sun', as a trope for the double stresses the optical and mediative bias of the phenomenon. The account impresses itself as inseparable from a rhetoric of perceptual aberration and trickery upon which it plays. The spectre is a double of the subject and a direct effect of the partial operation of the subject's body as medium in peculiar atmospheric effects. But whereas Brewster attempts to demystify magical properties of the Brocken Spectre, De Quincey emphasises it as optical phenomenon produced by the body, any-body. A process of demystification has already been performed by Brewster for De Quincey. Thus, what De Quincey does is to reconfigure its optional determinates by trope and analogy. The subject's body as medium provides a pertinent transition from monocular to stereoscopic mediation.

The historical transition from monocular mastery through the specularity as exhibited by the Spectre and to the shifting focus of stereoscopic mediation finds an important correspondence in Patmore's re-inscription of Wordsworth's 'The thorn'. Indeed, Patmore's 'The woodman's daughter' disrupts the entrenched monocular mastery in Wordsworth's poem. Whereas Wordsworth's text dramatises a specular relationship, Patmore's poem engenders a stereoscopic depth of field – which is further problematically articulated in Millais's painting The woodman's daughter. 'The thorn' concerns the tale of Martha Ray in the first-person narration of a retired 'captain of a small trading vessel' who has come to live on 'an annuity or small independent income in a village or country town of which he was not a native'.[17] The text arose from Wordsworth's desire to arrest a visual effect from his direct observation: 'on the ridge of Quantock Hill, on a stormy day, a thorn which [he] had often passed in calm and bright weather without noticing it' (Wordsworth, 1952, 2, p. 511). Martha Ray, as abandoned lover of Stephen Hill, is the object of entrenched superstition, which the rhetoric of the speaker perpetuates.

The mystery surrounding the fate of Martha Ray's illegitimate child represents, in the manner of 'The woodman's daughter', that which is withheld by the text, an absence fashioned by visible landmarks. In 'The thorn', the speaker repeatedly invites the reader to 'view', 'eye', 'trace', and 'espy' a configuration of 'aged thorn', 'little muddy pond', and 'hill of moss', and the sixth stanza articulates in the conditional the sighting of these: 'Now would you see this aged thorn,/This pond and beauteous hill of moss,/You must take care and chuse your time/The mountain when to cross' (11.5–8). The same stanza delineates as an object to visual perception 'a woman in a scarlet cloak' (1.62). But in the tenth stanza the speaker entreats the reader to enter a visual quest:

> I wish that you would go:
> Perhaps when you are at that place
> You something of her tale may trace. (11.107–9)

Here the containment of Martha's Ray's tale in topographically specific visible signs serves a similar function to the freshly-cut characters of the gibbet mast episode of Book XI of *The prelude*. Both are viewed by wanderers. In the gibbet mast episode a paradoxical notion of permanent inscription in turf is foregrounded by the method of its reappearance before the eye. The 'grass is cleared away' to reveal, by its absence, the presence of writing within a mutable medium. 'Superstition of the neighbourhood' is here the occasion of a re-inscription which involves a subtraction of nature as turf (Wordsworth, *The prelude* . . . , xi, 1.295–9). But by contrast, 'The thorn' presents 'the spot' to which Martha Ray 'goes' as a locale open to perceptual aberration.

It is stanza 17 of 'The thorn' which shifts emphasis to a reported sighting by the speaker who takes to the scene a telescope; a monocular instrument thus generates an occasion of perceptual aberration in which the eye's potential mastery is inverted.

> Twas mist and rain, and storm and rain
> No screen, no fence, could I discover,
> And then the wind! in faith, it was
> A wind full ten times over.
> I looked around, I thought I saw
> A jutting crag, and off I ran,
> Head-foremost, through the driving rain,
> The shelter of the crag to gain,
> And, as I am a man,
> Instead of a jutting crag, I found
> A woman seated on the ground. (11.187–97)

The poem here delineates as dramatic spectacle the process by which under certain atmospheric conditions an object may be seen to radically transform itself before the eye. Inextricable from this duping of the eye is an overturning of the whole authority of a single lensed medium, its inability to elucidate depth of field in the manner of the two eyes of stereopsis. Moreover, the text significantly withholds a physical description of Martha Ray: 'I did not speak – I saw her face, / Her face it was enough for me' (11.198–9). As a site for the struggle for perceptual mastery, the face assumes an enticing status which is re-figured by Patmore – and radically problematised by Millais.

In Patmore's 'The woodman's daughter' (1844), Maud replaces Martha and the squire's son Gerald becomes the Stephen Hill of 'The thorn'. There is a similar correlation of forsaken woman, subsequent pregnancy, illegitimate child, madness, and concealed murder/disappearance of child. However, Patmore's text does not find these events easily narratable and chronology is frustrated from the first stanza. The reader is incorporated by visual tropes and specifically by the invitation to look, 'the shadow of her shame and her/Deep in the stream behold!' (Patmore, C., ll. 73–4). *Shadow* here works both as a projection (evidence) and as a double (reflected) image. Indeed, Maud's grief which 'she may not avow' (1.130) equates with a disavowal of perceptual standpoint (vantage point); optical specificity is fashioned by inversion, by references to absent and failing sight. A 'dull pond' impresses itself initially as a non-reflectant. But Maud 'marks the closing weeds that shut/The water from her sight' (11.85–6), performing a desire to check/verify a completion of her act by optical authority. And here there occurs a process by which a mythically charged (narcissistic) reflective surface is rendered opaque. The myth of the double as 'parhelion' in both Brewster and De Quincey is rewritten by Patmore as a staging of a different optical bias, an indeterminate depth of field. By contrast 'The thorn' articulates an occasion of blatant specularity, an image of 'a baby and a baby's face' from within the 'pond' which 'looks at you,/When e'er you look on it, tis plain/the baby looks at you again' (11.227–30). This uncannily mismatched specular structure becomes in Patmore a fluctuating depth of field. The 'pool' of 'The woodman's daughter' shares the opacity of that of 'The thorn,' but the former as disturbed by 'weeds' reproblematises the staging of depth. For the water becomes emphatically a manipulatable site of optical debate.

Is it the twisting water – eft
That dimples the green slime? (11.95–6)

And again,

But Maud will never go
While those great bubbles struggle up
From the rotting weeds below (11.100–2)

Moreover the final stanza re-establishes the pool as a cardinal point of the debate. 'The night blackens the pool; but Maud/Is constant at her post' (11.110–11). Thus the return of a look to itself from the depth of Wordsworth's pond assumes in Patmore's pool a resolution into stereographic separations. It is a cultural shift from Romantic to Victorian inscriptions of optical agency.

Millais's *The woodman's daughter* (1850–1) **(12)** foregrounds both the position of a Victorian stereoscopically-empowered beholder and the agency of depth of field. If stereoscopy's mastery of, or authority on, the depth of field is present in the painting, then one might expect initially any condition of perceptual aberration or tricking of the eye (any visual 'slip') to be resolved. Yet this is not so. Instead, the painting calls attention to depth of field as the site of visual and cultural struggle. Submitted to the Royal Academy in 1851, together with two other of his works *Mariana* (Makins Collection) and *The return of the dove to the ark* (Ashmolean Museum, Oxford), *The woodman's daughter* was by far the most unpopular of the three and remained unsold at the close of the exhibition.[18] It was eventually bought by Millais's half-brother, Henry Hodgkinson. Critical commentary maintains that 'the problem was probably the face of the girl . . . Her original appearance is not a matter for conjecture, since Millais re-painted her face and other parts of the work at Henry Hodgkinson's request in 1886.' It is curious the manner in which art criticism has appropriated the occasion of the re-painting in order to dismiss it. As Malcolm Warner writes, the re-painting 'explains the *pentimenti* that are clearly visible in the picture, especially around the children's heads' (*The Pre-Raphaelites*, p. 87). But, one might ask, does it not rather conflate the re-painting of 1886 with that which occurred during its production of 1850 and 1851? It is useful to reintroduce the question in order to elucidate the way in which the re-painting works to suppress or contain potentially disruptive intertextual emphases, especially those of photography. It reminds us that the relationship of the Pre-Raphaelites to photography was a touchy subject from the outset, in part owing to the charge against which Ruskin defended the Brotherhood, of having painted over photographs. In itself this fact is worth noting. For the charge of painting over photographs draws our attention to an interesting, and, at this point, newly possible practice. What, we might ask, does a desire for exemption from this accusation imply? That the

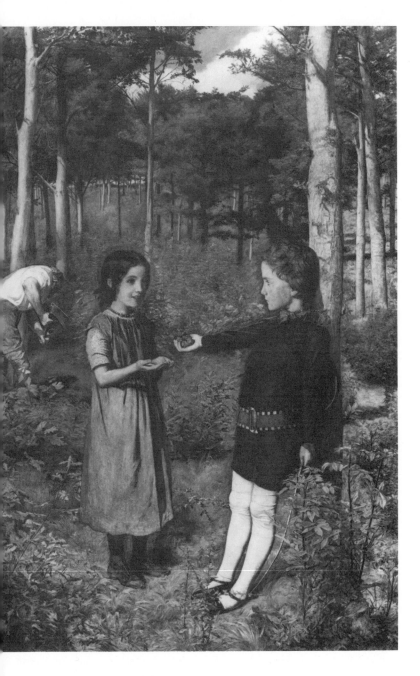

12 J. E. Millais, *The woodman's daughter*

photograph is capable of reproducing a greater accuracy which painting may utilise if its traces are buried, or rather if it conceals the traces of its dependency on the medium? One might then propose a particularised distinction between photography and painting: that painting is at liberty to conceal its uses of photography, whereas photography is unable by way of its historical or retrospective reference to conceal its uses of painting. Another question then arises. Are attempts by photography to imitate painting less easily concealed precisely because photography completely redefines the trompe l'oeil of painting? Moreover, is the trompe l'oeil of photography closer to a dompte regard? Does the stereoscopic photograph attempt to tame rather than to trick the eye?[19]

A rhetoric of the ruined face operates strategically to contain subversive elements of the painting and of its relationship to Patmore's poem, to divert criticism from other, potentially political, topical concerns. Moreover, a failure to address the culturally significant question of depth of field is indicative of the way in which art criticism has preferred to avoid or to suppress intertextuality even when, as here, it posits itself as a blatant correspondence in image and text of the same title. In other words, criticism, I believe, re-casts a potentially disruptive relationship of The woodman's daughter(s) (Millais's to Patmore's) in order to forget the painting's origins in a culturally specific and politically charged optical debate. It is significant that the repainting occurs in a second wave of stereo-mania in Britain.[20] Patmore's comment (just prior to the re-painting of the girl's face) that 'the girl looked like a vulgar little slut' not only positions The woodman's daughter as a far cry from his The angel in the house (1854), for which he is chiefly remembered, but also constitutes a further gesture towards suppression – Patmore's self-estrangement from intertextual concerns which his own poem had generated.[21]

Thus I am arguing that there evolves a conspiracy to contain (to render opaque so to speak) the elusive depth of field of Millais's painting. This is all the more interesting when contemporary comments posit its articulation of depth as singularly well-handled. M. H. Spielman records that 'the charge of flatness – as though it had been passed through a mangle – which had been brought against Lorenzo and Isabella (13), had so stirred Millais that he resolved to produce in his next work [Christ in the house of his parents] a picture in which light and shade and pronounced projection should confound his critics'. And we are told that this was the 'motive' of Millais's sudden change of manner. It is thus significant that The woodman's daughter (12) was begun while Christ in the house of his parents was on the easel, while 'pronounced projection' remained a new incentive for Millais. Moreover, William Millais's discussion of the woodland context painted on location in Oxford further draws attention to the staging of relief:

I think perhaps the most beautiful background ever painted by my brother is to be found in his picture of The woodman's daughter . . . Eye cannot follow the mysterious interlacing of all the wonderful things that spring up all about, where every kind of wood growth seems to be striving to get the upper hand and to reach the sunlight first, where every leaf and tendril stands out in bold relief. (Millais, 1, pp. 110–11)

However, when William Millais discusses the figures of the painting, its strategies appear increasingly duplicitous:

Every blade of grass, every leaf and branch, and every shadow that they cast in the sunny wood is presented here with unflinching realism and infinite delicacy of detail. Yet the figures are in no way swamped by their surroundings, every accessory taking its proper place, in subordination to the figures and the tale they have to tell. (Millais, 1, pp. 109–10)

The transcription of the whole is here described as rendering objects in equal degrees of intensity, and yet all are said to remain subordinate to the domination of the figures. William Holman Hunt cites 'the head of the boy in The woodman's daughter, the effect of sunlight on flesh' to demonstrate his and Millais's independent development of the technique of 'painting over a ground of wet white' (Hunt, 1905, 1, p. 276). For the most part, however, criticism splits discussion into two parts: the unprecedented accuracy in the handling of landscape depth, and the failure in the painting of the girl's head. And even William Millais, although preferring its original state, pronounces the head 'rustic' prior to its ruin (Millais, 1, p. 98). However, the implied incompatibility of figure and ground finds a productive metaphor in the cultural/theoretical impact of a newly articulated third dimension. The link of The woodman's daughter with aspects of photographic discourse is obvious. Millais's anecdotes concerning the 'real' out of season strawberries bought from Covent Garden for an inflated price (as reported by Arthur Hughes) and the request for authentic country girl's 'smock' and 'worn boots' lend to the painting a modified version of the photograph's 'having been there'. Moreover Michael Bartram points out that 'putting children in woodland scenes was a common photographic practice', and there are, of course, treatments in painting roughly contemporary with that of Millais such as 'Hughes's The woodman's child of 1860. But these observations fail to engage questions of the infinitely problematic depth of field. Millais's painting dramatises stereoscopic mediation as the most interesting vehicle for perceptual aberration, for the eyes' unrest, primarily because one imagines its enticing articulation of depth to constitute an assurance in relation to the potentially troubling depth of field. And yet Millais's painting, by way of its resolution into stereoscopic planes, calls attention to the contingency of depth as optical struggle, just as Patmore's poem depends for its secrecy upon a unique staging and 'upstaging' of visual tropes.

In many ways, it is the re-painting of the face which calls attention to the painting's representation of the look, and in the articulation of depth in the exchange between the two figures there is an odd suggestion of monocular and stereoscopic methods. The girl's look is uncanny; in one sense it appears to be that of a front elevation and a profile. Its angle is oddly proportioned, reaching both out towards and beyond the boy, thus problematising the condition of depth. There is therefore created between the two children an elusive depth of field, an indeterminate relationship of her vantage point to the vanishing point of her line of sight, fixed elsewhere. Thus her gaze, in part, engenders the stereoscopic effect in the body's spatial relationship to her. There is an odd relationship of the girl's features to the positioning of her body, a sense that where more appropriately the beholder might expect one of the eyes to be visible there appear the two eyes required by stereopsis. The painting thereby dramatises the potential disturbances of the two-eyed look.

The girl's gaze positions the boy after her line of sight, and thereby contributes to a stereographic effect. In other words, it is not only the articulation of stereoscopic depth in the painting which becomes problematic, but also the fact that the interchange between the figures, as represented in the look, becomes a signature for the staging of the third dimension. Rather than focusing upon him and becoming a look returned or met, the girl's look is a look beyond and is not returned. The boy thereby becomes a prominent plane in the stereoscopic effect to which, of course, the opposition of the complementaries red and green contributes. What continues to be unsettling about the painting is exactly this mobilisation of this depth of field, an enactment of optical strategy as perpetually aberrant. The boy becomes positioned by her look as an intermediate plane, a screen between her and an undisclosed object of her gaze. It is as if, then, the face as the site at which Millais continued to struggle foregrounds the essential intervolvement of Pre-Raphaelitism and stereoscopy and becomes itself a metaphor for the political rivalry between monocular and stereoscopic mediation.

'Monoscopy', with its implied emphasis upon a single-eyed vision, attempts to appropriate the powers of sight for a critically privileged elite.

Stereoscopy, on the other hand, with its mass appeal and its production within popular culture, threatens, by way of photography, that hierarchical structure, derived as it is from the identification of monocular instruments with the singular and supreme authority of the artist's perception. Therefore dismissal of the stereoscope in the light of its mass popularity reveals a political bias correlative with the disapproval that initially greeted Pre-Raphaelitism. It was here that Ruskin made his celebrated intervention. In both cases, a dismissal of two-eyed vision in favour of monoscopy, by implication, suppresses popular culture as it serves to legitimise a ruling elite. Indeed, in Millais's painting the obvious class difference between squire's son and woodman's daughter reproduces simultaneously this same class struggle in optical terms.

The critical debate centred upon Pre-Raphaelitism therefore contains within itself a 'larger' cultural and political struggle for the role of the artist, the critic, and the beholder. These are issues that the age-old equation of Pre-Raphaelitism with photographic 'realism' completely glosses over, thereby protecting art criticism from engagement in a radically intertextual discourse. Thus, to restore to view the specificity of a single instrument, the stereoscope, and its ramifications as inseparable from the discourse of Pre-Raphaelitism is to dramatise how a deconstruction of the myth of photographic exactitude reveals the means by which monoscopy perpetuates its dominance.

Notes

1 Take for example, Alan Bowness's remark in a footnote to the introduction to *The Pre-Raphaelites*, p. 12: 'In a perceptive phrase, Geoffrey Grigson once said that the Pre-Raphaelites surrounded themselves for posterity "with a set of gigantic magnifying glasses".' The purpose to which Bowness puts this remark demonstrates precisely the manner in which art history perpetuates the use of optical discourse as throwaway analogy.

2 The invention of the stereoscope in 1832 led to the reformulation of accounts of illusionism. The phenomenon of binocular vision depends upon each eye viewing the object from a slightly different angle. Separate images received by each eye are converted by the brain into a single image. As far as I know this connection between stereoscopy and Pre-Raphaelitism has previously gone unnoticed.

3 To dramatise one example of this identification I cite the Dublin photographer James Robinson, who represents a crucial intervolvement of Pre-Raphaelite painting, photography and the law. In a stereographic series on the poet Chatterton, his inclusion of a scene staged in precise imitation of Henry Wallis's painting *Chatterton* (1855–56) had telling and unprecedented legal consequences. In 1859, Robert Turner, the owner of the engraving rights, brought a successful injunction against Robinson and it was established that a photographic mock-up of a painting was equivalent in copyright terms to an engraving, or to a photograph of the painting itself. The copyright issue here may be read

as an attempt to contain/retard subversive implications of the newly mobilised third dimension of the stereo photograph. For a side-by-side reproduction of the painting and the photograph, see Bartram, p. 156 and Greenhill, pp. 199–205.

4 It is here productive to take into account contemporary reviews of the first volume of Pre-Raphaelite poetry, William Morris's *The defence of Guenevere and other poems* (1858), since they conspire to bring together Pre-Raphaelite painting, optical instruments and photography in the belief that their conjunction provides an unquestionably derogatory analogy. See especially: Unsigned Review, the *Saturday review*, 20 November 1858, p. 507, 'When painters think it their duty to work through a microscope . . .', and Unsigned notice, the *Spectator* XXXI, Feb. 1858, p. 238, and Unsigned notice, the *Athenaeum*, no. 1588, 3 April 1858, pp. 427–8.

5 N. Niepce invented the technique of heliography (sun drawing) in 1822, taking the first photograph of nature from his attic window in 1826, on a pewter plate with an exposure time of approximately eight hours. For a detailed discussion of Niepce's invention and a history of photographic processes, see Gernsheim.

6 Accounts of the Romantic sublime are central to this shift. See Landow, 1971 and Helsinger. What is crucial here is Ruskin's departure from the artist's response to the visible as a model for less 'privileged' spectators. A departure from the 'Romantic sublime and its imperatives' inheres in Ruskin's 'noble' or 'Turnerian picturesque'. As Helsinger writes, 'Ruskin puts the beholder before the artist as his model for the reform of perception that he saw as essential to the nineteenth century' (p. 71).

7 In a letter to Mrs Cowper-Temple, referring to Ezekiel, 24:16, Ruskin writes 'the worst of me is that the Desire of the Eyes is so much more to me! Ever so much more than the desire of the mind.' Quoted in Fellows, p. viii.

8 On the subject of magnifying glasses and for Ruskin's advice to a 'rose queen' see Ruskin, 14, p. 408, and 30, p. 346.

9 Hewison writes of the Claude-glass: 'the reflected image compressed the real view and reduced the brilliance of its colour to appear more like a painting' (p. 1).

10 See Ruskin, 26, pp. 114–15, 262.

11 Gernsheim, pp. 253–62. See also Wheatstone, 1838. One problem with Wheatstone's stereoscope was that it required large-format photographs which kept the cost high.

12 Claudet, A., 'Photography in its relation to the fine arts', *The photographic journal*, vol. 6, 15 June 1860.

13 *The stereoscopic magazine: a gallery of landscape scenery, architecture, antiquities, and natural history, accompanied with descriptive articles by writers of eminence*, London, 1858. Published monthly, price 2s 6d, and printed under the superintendence of James Glaisher, the magazine ran from 1 July 1858 to February 1865.

14 Of course the *carte-de-visite* achieved enormous popularity, and it instigated the fashion for collecting photographs in albums. 'Cartomania' was an international phenomenon. It became the custom of friends to exchange *cartes*, and those of public figures were termed 'sure cards' because of the huge demand for them. Although *carte*-size landscapes are the forerunners of the picture-postcard, it is important to note that as such they were not introduced into England until 1901.

The *carte* differs from the stereograph because, on the one hand, it substitutes portraits for narratives and foreign scenes, and, on the other hand, it eliminates the need for an instrument of mediation. In this sense, it does not contain the stereoscope's potential to expose the workings of monoscopy as a dominant social practice.

15 Brewster, *The stereoscope* . . . , p. 1. Not only does Brewster stress for the instrument a unique credibility in its relationship to phenomena, but he creates for it elaborate educational/cultural roles. It is significant to compare Brewster's text on the stereoscope with that of his earlier invention, the kaleidoscope. The kaleidoscope is of course distinguished by its monocular and exclusively recreational function, its somewhat arbitrary production of endlessly different symmetries. See, Brewster, 1819. Brewster was

ruthless in his attitude to optical inventions and he had few qualms about demolishing the reputations of fellow scientists. This is evident in his attempts to disprove Wheatstone's invention of the first stereoscope and in his attitude to John Fearn's work on cerebral vision. See *The stereoscope*, pp. 21–33, and Fearn, 1837.

16 De Quincey, *Suspiria de profundis*, originally published in *Blackwood's Edinburgh Magazine*, 1845, in De Quincey, ed. Lindop, p. 156. De Quincey directs his reader to Brewster's text as 'the best scientific comment' on the Spectre (note p. 153). As De Quincey writes of the production of the 'apparition of the Brocken': 'At first, from the distance and the colossal size, every spectator supposes the appearance to be quite independent of himself. But very soon he is surprised to observe his own motions and gestures mimicked: and wakens to the conviction that the phantom is but a dilated reflection of himself' (note p. 153). However, in the manner of De Quincey's 'dark interpreter', who 'sometimes mixes with alien natures', the Spectre does not take part in a simple relationship of specularity, but is 'sometimes disturbed by storms or by driving showers, so as to dissemble his real origin' (p. 156).

17 Wordsworth, 1952, vol. 2, p. 512. 'The thorn', composed in March and April 1798, appeared that year in *Lyrical Ballads*.

18 *The Pre-Raphaelites*, p. 86. Spielman, p. 89, and Millais, pp. 98–9. In addition see Millais, p. 92, for a reproduction of a pencil study of *The woodman's daughter* executed prior to the alteration of the face.

19 I here take the terms from Jacques Lacan, 'Of the gaze as objet petit a', Lacan, *The four fundamental concepts* . . . The distinction Lacan makes between the workings of *trompe l'oeil* and *dompte regard* most effectively articulates the problematics of depth of field in relation to perspective systems, particularly geometral. Thus in one sense the relationship of stereoscopic photography to painting dramatises the difference between a 'taming' and a 'duping' of the eye.

20 A second wave of stereoscopic photography began in England in 1887, largely owing to the work of W. I. Chadwick of the Manchester Photographic Society. But by the outbreak of the First World War it had again died out (Gernsheim, p. 259).

21 Patmore, C., letter to F. G. Stephens, 30 November 1885, quoted by Warner, *The Pre-Raphaelites*, p. 86.

6

Histories of matrimony:
J. E. Millais
Marcia Pointon

On 2 December 1850, John Everett Millais wrote to Mrs Combe, wife of one of his patrons and a regular friend and correspondent, 'My dear Mrs. Pat, – First I thank you most intensely for the Church Service. The night of its arrival I read the marriage ceremony for the first time in my life, and shall look upon every espoused man with awe' (Millais, 1, p. 89). The popularity for Victorian artists both of the subject of matrimony, and of its obverse, the unmarried woman, has been frequently remarked upon. Casteras devotes a chapter of her recent book to courtship and marriage (Casteras, 1987, ch. 6) while Roberts draws attention to Richard Redgrave's series of paintings on the plight of the 'redundant woman', she who is 'compelled to lead an independent and incomplete existence' of her own (Roberts, p. 57). These were the seamstresses whose condition Millais addressed much later in his life in Stitch! Stitch! of 1876 and Virtue and vice, a drawing dated 1853 showing an underpaid needlewoman being tempted into prostitution.[1]

Millais, like his contemporaries, was aware of the prominent place allocated to matrimony and its lack in cultural production, from the iconography of the mystic marriage of St Catherine to the Book of Common Prayer with its authoritative words of command. The members of the Pre-Raphaelite Brotherhood are often presented as an avant-garde movement in opposition to their time (e.g. Rose, pp. 4–5). Moreover, the paintings of the early 'Pre-Raphaelite' period of 1849 to 1860 are seen as differing from later work by those same artists.[2] These definitions not only obscure continuing thematisation in works that are stylistically distinct from the so-called 'Pre-Raphaelite' works but also serve to blur the commonality of interest between Pre-Raphaelite artists and their contemporaries. In this chapter I shall be examing imagery relating, whether positively or negatively, to matrimony in the work of J. E. Millais. Fundamental to my argument will be the premise that paintings do not reflect a given social reality exterior to them but are themselves a discursive practice. Therefore this chapter is not a documentary account of marriage as illustrated in art. It is an examination of how the ideology of marriage – marriage as institution, regulation, theory and practice – is the matrix around which a sequence of images by Millais can be seen to signify. In other words imagery is seen to operate as a defining process, unifying, obscuring and linking fictions in the production and enforcement of ideology. To concentrate on one artist is not to imply an unproblematic link between artist and painting or drawing; Millais has been chosen for this study because his work is open to examination through intertextuality, allowing for the unpacking of notions about iconography, social history, biography and style which remain the dominant strands of art-historical method. Marriage in this chapter is proposed as a problematic; Millais's imagery is one site where the conflicts and contradictions that make up that problematic can be examined.

We might begin by asking what a representation of a marriage might look like. Marriage has for several centuries in the West been construed as, at one and the same time, a ceremony and a ritual, a personal condition, an economic unit, a legally defined state and an uncoded but widely recognised set of expectations. It is, as many have observed, fraught with contradictions. In particular this still normative union remains the only legal contract which requires the partners to be of the opposite sex and, unlike commercial contracts, the parties are limited in the terms they can introduce into the agreement.

There can be no bargaining between spouses since the State decrees what marriage shall be. It is not, in fact, a contract between the spouses, but rather they agree together to accept a certain (externally defined) status. This is because marriage is regarded by both church and state as a 'natural institution', of unquestioned form, to which they merely give support and blessing'. (Barker, p. 254)

Most contradictory is the fact that this 'coming together' in the sight of the Church and State serves to underline and reinforce gender distinctions. Marriage involves very different social and legal requirements, rights and expectations for a man than for a woman. It is also the dominant state for a woman but not, necessarily, for a man. The celibate woman is to be explained and defined with reference to marriage. Most contradictory of all is the attempt in Western society to integrate eroticism with legitimate marriage as a 'ceremony followed by intercourse' (Barker, p. 249). Simone de Beauvoir, with typical acumen, remarked that 'to reconcile marriage and love is such a *tour de force* that nothing less than divine intervention is required for success' (de Beauvoir, p. 457).

The solemnisation of marriage service that Millais read for the first time in 1850 is a very different text than the one which most couples marrying in the Anglican Church today encounter; it is both longer and more specific in its frame of reference and in its examples. It is grounded in authority and the law. Adam and Eve, the first married pair, are cited (though not their subsequent misfortunes) and, most formidable, the state of marriage is offered as an analogue to the unity between Christ and his Church. In the words of St Paul and St Peter, men are exhorted to honour their wives as weaker vessels and wives to obey and submit to their husbands. This textual authority, whether acknowledged or not, underpins all discourses of marriage and establishes an unquestioned, if unstable law, against which the practices and experiences of marriage are represented and measured.

We talk of such and such a film, book, or play as being 'a portrait of a marriage'. But what we are invariably thinking of is a representation more or less fragmentary of a situation in which two people coexist. The iconography of mid-Victorian paintings may allude to the dependency of wives or the economic responsibilities of husbands, but the abstract concept of matrimony, whether as state legislation or as religious sacrament, is always more than the particular imagined event or events, prevalent as ideology and as discourse but never *simply* linked to illustration. Nonetheless, we are concerned with a particular historical moment in which regulations and expectations around matrimony across virtually the whole class spectrum in Britain were in the process of articulation and crystallisation. And again, the implications for men were different from those for women. (Best, p. 97).

Marriage, as we still know it, was legally constituted first in Lord Hardwicke's Act of 1753, but it was the 1836 Marriage Act, followed by a Births and Deaths Registration Act, which brought into existence local Superintendent Registrars and the centralised system of state registration of marriage. For the first time since the Middle Ages it was possible for anyone to contract a fully valid marriage by civil ceremony. Whilst marriage was (and still is) an easy contract to make, it was virtually impossible to break (Barker, pp. 243–7). The crucial years in divorce law reform were 1857 to 1878 but, as is now well known, women's rights in these matters, especially in relation to custody of children and control of property, remained minimal and highly problematic (Best, pp. 302–3; Holcomb, pp. 4–22).

Gillis has described how what he terms 'domestic republicanism' was halted by the 1840s and how, during the period 1850 to 1960, there was a retreat from marriage as partnership. 'Even as heterosexual possibilities narrowed and monogamous marriage became virtually mandatory, the conditions for satisfactory conjugal relations became ever more problematic' (p. 233). Whilst the Marriage Act allowed for choices in official forms of marriage (registry office, nonconformist chapel, church and so on) the enforcement of existing law became much more rigorous and the kinds of 'folk' marriages and widely recognised arrangements both for cohabitation and divorce that were commonplace in the eighteenth century were outlawed. As so often in the enforcement of legislation, it was the middle classes who were most immediately affected by the pressure for conformity, the upper classes possessing the means to by-pass the law either physically (by travelling abroad when necessary) or by financial inducement, and the lower classes suffering less by virtue of the survival, albeit in reduced form, of some of the accepted alternatives to marriage and divorce. Gillis points out that the new legislation was tied up with the poor law reform of 1834, and was part of a more general effort by a triumphant bourgeoisie to improve the machinery of the State and, through it, to control the lives of the poor (p. 239). But the law itself is, suggests Gillis, not a sufficient explanation for the new compulsion to marriage; he proposes as the single greatest factor 'the evolution of industrial capitalism, which undermined the independence of the family economy and consigned to men the role of breadwinner and to women the destiny of dependent wife and mother' (pp. 241–2). For women, marriage came to constitute the sole point of access to adult life; girlhood was therefore a period of preparation for marriage.

The identification of girlhood as a privileged place in relation to the entry into marriage will be seen to be of particular significance in relation to Millais's images of bridesmaids. If marriage as discourse predicates the wifely state as dependent, then the unmarried but marriageable girl (most readily culturally identifiable in the person of the bridesmaid) must be shown to have choice whilst simultaneously being shown to be without choice since, marriage demanding subordination not companionate equality, an independent girl is by her nature unmarriageable. It is this conundrum which will be one of the focuses of attention in our examination of Millais's hypostatisation of the bridesmaid.

Before turning to Mallais, I want to draw attention to the fact that it is precisely in the years when the compulsion to marriage was so prevalent, from the late 1840s through to the 1850s, that marriage features directly or indirectly as a prominent discourse in Millais's paintings as well as in works by other members of the Brotherhood. It is also important to recognise that the connection between poor law legislation and the Marriage Act to which Gillis draws attention was merely the external manifestation of the attempt to regulate the role of marriage in the labour market; marriage for middle-class men like Millais effectively meant their labour was required as of compulsion, not of choice. Finally, the insistence on the heterosexual nature of marriage institutionalised and enforced by discourse and within culture should be noted; the production of paintings featuring marriageable young women has to be seen in the context of the intimacy between young men. For the young artists of the Brotherhood in 1849 the contradictions inherent in the concept of marriage were a condition of middle-class existence; the discourse of romantic love which they identified in Boccaccio, Ariosto, Keats and Tennyson (see, for example, Rossetti's poem, published in The germ in 1850 on Ingres's painting based on Ariosto's poem, or Millais's Isabella of 1849 from Boccaccio) had to be accommodated alongside the mystic marriage of St Catherine (also the subject of one of Rossetti's 1850 sonnets) and the daunting text of the marriage ceremony.

In their own lives these contradictions were writ large. Effie Ruskin's annulment legally returned her to the condition of Euphemia Gray, but socially the marriage could not so easily be undone. One manifestation of this contradiction is to be seen in the way that Effie's lack of visibility in the London social world – the world her husband continued to frequent during the early years of their marriage – is matched by her extraordinary visibility in Millais's major paintings, for which she virtually invariably posed as the model. Rossetti's tortuous indecision about marrying his lover, Elizabeth Siddall, is indicative of conflicts around class and economic interest. For middle-class women and men the definition of marriage as economic unit was experienced with a particular resonance (Davidoff and Hall). Jane Burden was reputedly in love with Dante Gabriel Rossetti, not William Morris, but married the latter at the behest of her family, as his wealthy background would ensure an unhoped-for degree of economic security for her relatives and the Rossetti family were known to have fallen on hard times (The Pre-Raphaelites, p. 170). Millais's wife was immediately subsumed into her husband's professional life, providing unpaid labour and proving an economic asset to her husband (M., Warner, 1985, p. 95). Millais embraced a work ethic as a direct consequence of marriage, writing to Holman Hunt on 1 February 1856: 'I have more than my own mouth to fill now, and I work, when otherwise [as a bachelor] I never should have thought of it'.[3]

Marriage and marriage-related themes are dominant in Millais's work throughout his life;[4] from his juvenile prize-winning *The Benjamites seizing their brides* and *The proposal* through *Cymon and Iphigenia* (from Boccaccio's story in which an uncouth swain is transformed by marriage), *The woodman's daughter* (a story of childhood love destined for disaster because of class incompatibility), *The order of release, 1746* (1852–53) and a series of paintings of bridesmaids, to *The bride* (c. 1858), *The gambler's wife* (RA, 1869), *Wedding cards: jilted* (pre-1855), and a sequence of drawings of the 1850s dealing with the theme of marriage and its rituals. If this rough list were extended to include those paintings in which marriage, by its absence, underpins a narrative of loss or lack, like *Mariana*, *Ophelia*, *The value of rest*, *Isabella*, *A Huguenot*, and those works which, as Grieve has pointed out (1976, pp. 31–2) deal with female fertility, like *Autumn leaves* and *Spring*, it would be a great deal longer.

The stylistic and iconographic roots of Millais's treatment of this theme lie with Hogarthian narrative and with French eighteenth-century paintings of sentiment. *The proposal* and *The gambler's wife*, both early works, testify to the influence of Fragonard and Chardin. The subject-matter also relates to Hogarth's *Marriage à la mode*. But these similarities must not be allowed to obscure for us the significant differences between Millais and the tradition to which he has long been recognised as belonging. It is within the deviations from that tradition that Millais's paintings signify. Millais's drawing *Married for money* (**16**) (1853) in which a dark-clad female figure dominates the foreground where she furtively observes from a gallery the marriage ceremony being conducted down below, relates compositionally to Hogarth's *The Wedding of Stephen Beckingham and Mary Cox* (**17**) (1729–30).[5] Hogarth's ceremony is observed by the two small figures who lean from the gallery; whilst not unimportant, they are relatively obscure and indeterminate, suggesting the world of the street and the public as it impinges upon the private ceremony of middle-class nuptials. What is significant is the way in which Millais inverts the composition, making the voyeur the dominant presence, the major figure via whose turned back the viewer enters the composition. Moreover, the cornucopia-carrying cherubs that Hogarth stations above the couple's heads, counteracting any negative connotations produced by the intrusive figures from the outside world, are notably absent in Millais's composition, which is thus ominous and dangerous. This quality of danger is reinforced by the telescoped and prison-like architectural setting; the participants are trapped between vertiginously receding architectural components in an interior space that contrasts markedly with Hogarth's

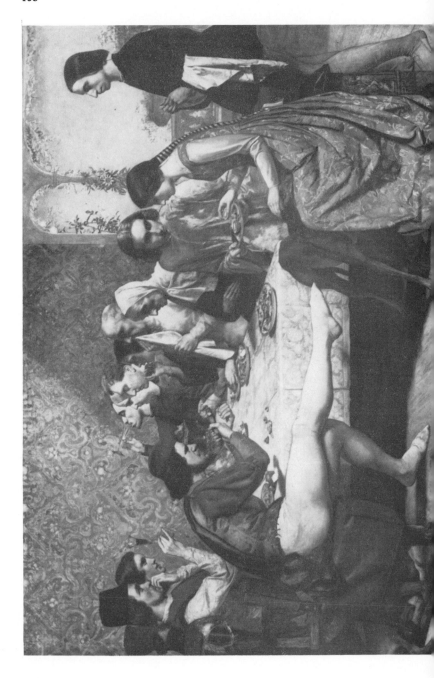

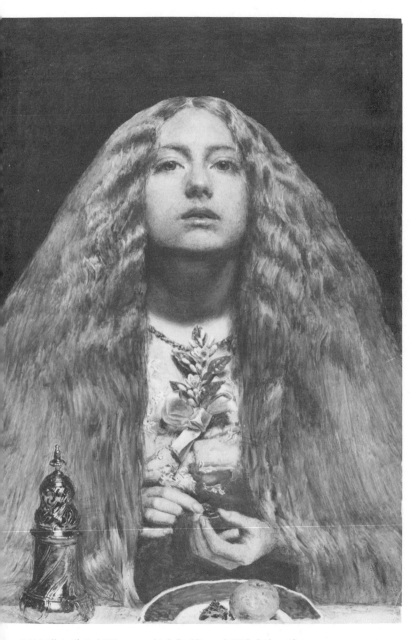

J. E. Millais: (facing) **13** *Lorenzo and Isabella*; (this page) **14** *The bridesmaid*

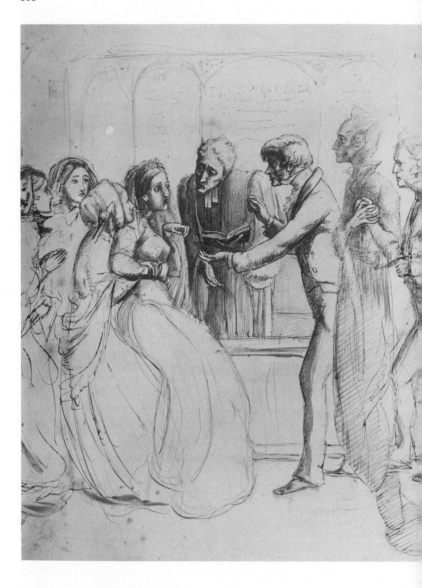

15 J. E. Millais, *A ghost appearing at a wedding ceremony*

facing
16 J. E. Millais, *Married for money*
17 W. Hogarth, *The wedding of Stephen Beckingham and Mary Cox*

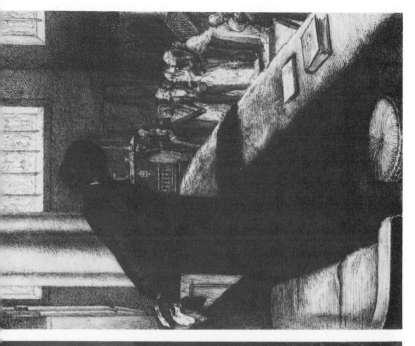

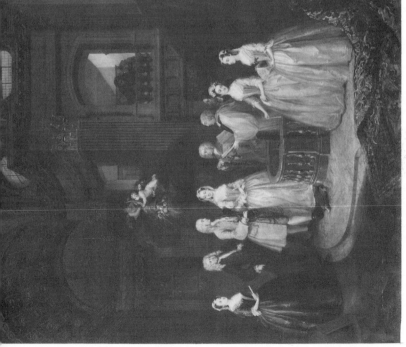

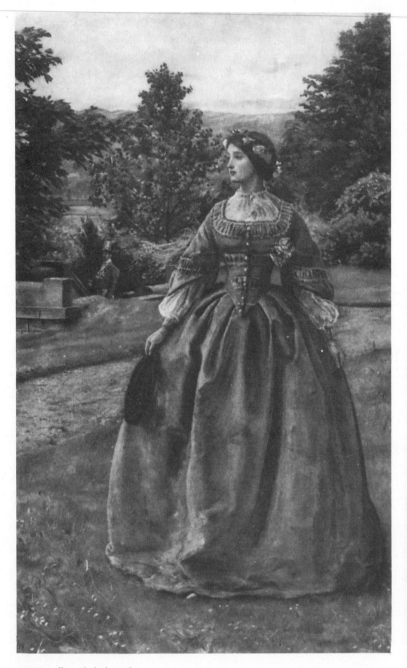

18 J. E. Millais, *The bridesmaid*

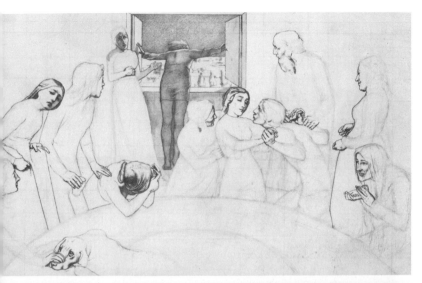

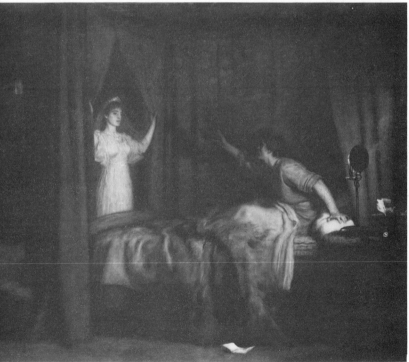

J. E. Millais: **19** The flood; **20** Speak! Speak!

elegant and light-filled interior.

Married for money (16) is one of a series of drawings executed in 1852–53 which have often been understood to be autobiographical. Evans argues that the drawing, A ghost appearing at a wedding ceremony (15), is a symbolic picture of Effie Gray's marriage to John Ruskin, drawn by Millais in 1853 after Effie had confided her troubles to him. John James Ruskin had committed suicide in a fit of insanity in the very house near Perth where Effie was born. The drawing is inscribed: 'I don't, I don't', and behind the parson the tablet above the altar bears the words: 'I believe in God the Father.' Evans interpreted these texts as referring to the aversion of the bride when she comes to the moment in the service when she has to say 'I do' and remembers the 'dark shadow of madness' that lay on the Ruskin family (p. 201).

Warner's recent examination of Millais's career to 1863 dismisses the biographical interpretation of this drawing (M. Warner, 1985, p. 490; The Pre-Raphaelites, no. 193), arguing that marriage subjects are common in Millais's work of the early 1850s and that such highly personal connotations would be quite exceptional. Evans's insistence upon a precisely illustrative function for the drawing A ghost appearing at a wedding ceremony and the dependency of her argument on the identification of the two protagonists as portraits of particular individuals is problematic. The drawing is one of a series. By isolating the ghost drawing Evans has obscured what is a repeated and insistent thematic underpinning of all the drawings. Moreover, the general disregard in which Millais's late work has been held has led to the artist's abiding concern with matrimonial themes being ignored. Most significantly his very late work, Speak! Speak! of 1895, (20) has been completely overlooked. In this large-scale work (66×83in.) the roles of Fuseli's celebrated The nightmare, with which Millais's painting has certain disturbing affinities, and the ghost drawing are reversed. Here a young man starts up in bed at the spectre of a bride who parts the curtains at the foot of the bed.

In his statement to Mrs Combe, Millais not only presents himself as a painter but also as a marriageable man. And marriage remains prominent in his agenda where it seems to have been irrevocably associated with menace, with overbearing authority and with a sinister oppression of the waking spirits. A Hogarthian breadth of vision in which marriage is one of many regulatory practices (see especially The rake's progress and Marriage à la mode), is telescoped in Millais's paintings and drawings to a series of discourses of form, function and symbol in ritual. It is perhaps not insignificant that the opening pages of The life and letters of Sir John Everett

Millais published by the artist's son in 1899 juxtapose a photograph of Millais's father, John William Millais, dressed as a monk against a theatrical back-cloth of rocks (*c*. 1870) and a passage describing the major role of his mother (his 'truest and most helpful friend') in the education of this artist who was never sent to school and who was wont to say in later years: 'I owe everything to my mother' (p. 3). The relegation of the father to a fancy-dress celibate hermit-figure might be seen, symbolically, to have removed all competition for the love of the mother. In such a relationship marriage is both intensely desired and, in Millais's own words, full of awe. The powerful wife/mother figure is the subject of *The order of release, 1746* where a woman carrying a sleeping child on one shoulder allows her Jacobite husband to bury his head on her other shoulder, while she hands the jailer the order of release mentioned in the title. *Peace concluded* of 1856, featuring the family of a soldier wounded in the Crimea, assigns a similar role to the wife/mother.

In Millais's first major painting after the formation of the Pre-Raphaelite Brotherhood, he depicted Lorenzo and Isabella from Boccaccio's story as retold by Keats in *Isabella: or the pot of basil* (**13**). Exhibited at the Royal Academy in 1849, it was accompanied by verses which unequivocally spell out the contradiction between romantic love (between daughter of the house and employee) and marriage as an economic unit. The strikingly original 'dinner party' scene depicted by Millais, with its relentless line of physiognomies leading to a richly decorated but depressingly blank wall and its daunting sense of alienation (only Lorenzo and Isabella communicate and their contact is clearly non-verbal) is the inverse of the family conviviality of hearth and home celebrated in Victorian painting and fiction. It is also a visible corruption of the eighteenth-century concept of a conversation piece and, indeed, of the sacred connection between eating, social intercourse and spirituality.

In December 1850, Millais was working on *Mariana* (based on Tennyson's poem) and on *The Woodman's daughter* (**12**) (based on a poem by Coventry Patmore) which, like *Lorenzo and Isabella* and *Ophelia* which he began late in 1851, deals with ill-fated affection between people of different classes (Grieve, 1976, pp. 23–4). By the following month he was reporting to Mrs Combe satisfactory progress on both paintings (which would be exhibited at the Royal Academy that summer). He also mentions three other works: 'The Nun', 'The Bridesmaid' and 'The Flood'. Despite its apparently unconnected title, *The flood* (**19**) is, as Grieve has pointed out (1976, p. 26), also a marriage subject; I shall return to this in due course. For the moment let us concentrate on the connections between The bridesmaid and the subject of the The nun, for the painting itself remains unlocated.[6]

The bride of Christ was of interest to Millais's companion of this period, Charles Allston Collins, who became a Roman Catholic and one of whose best-known works is Convent thoughts of 1850–51. Grieve has established a general interest in High Anglicanism and Roman Catholicism among the Pre-Raphaelite artists at this time (Grieve, 1969). Moreover, Rossetti's sister, Maria, whom Collins wished to marry, entered the High Anglican community attached to All Saints, Margaret Street. But Millais is generally regarded as an essentially secular artist and it is, therefore, worth examining the appearance of the nun in his work. Millais's two renderings of St Agnes's eve establish a binary relationship between the two brides, the secular and the religious. In 1849 he depicted, in a frankly erotic study, Madeline standing in her chamber with her outer garments falling from her in a heap on the floor. The study was finally used for a painting in 1862–63. Represented thus, neither a naked model nor a clothed woman, the figure of Madeline is highly provocative. Clothing as social practice defines the boundaries between nature and culture, and the act of divesting the clothing is an act of avowal in the physical, a declaration of the body. It is the sight of the empty dress, after all that entranced Porphyro in Keats's poem. Such a reading would have been reinforced for a contemporary audience by the knowledge of Madeline as Magdalen, the biblical prostitute. Four years later Millais produced a finished drawing of St Agnes's eve by Tennyson portraying a nun looking out of a window over snow-covered convent roofs. Whilst the poem on which it is based essentially concerns the spiritual marriage of the bride of Christ, the title links it to the secular rendering. Moreover, as Malcolm Warner has indicated (The Pre-Raphaelites, no. 200) the drawing is implicated in Millais's own history, since it is based on a sketch for a proposed portrait of Effie made in 1853 and the face of the nun was observed by Effie to be a self-portrait of the artist.

The nun provided a solution to the Pre-Raphaelite debate about history and the modern life subject (as manifest in the Germ in March and May 1850). For the nun is neither of the past, nor of the present, and being outside the secular social is also outside secular time. Exercising power by refusal of heterosexuality in the marriage bond (and the paradigm here must be Measure for measure), a woman living among women, the nun is an object of fantasy and desire in art and literature of the period. The history of the St Agnes' eve drawing suggests that Millais brought together his own image and that of Effie in a representation of frozen chastity, a sort of negative union.[7] The idea of the nun is, therefore, not in opposition to matrimony but inscribed within it. The nun enables the concept of virginal timelessness to survive within the ideal of marriage. This is borne out in the fact that The Vale of rest, Millais's most celebrated painting of nuns (1858), was the consequence of a romantic vision on the part of Millais and Effie on their honeymoon and was later spoken of by the artist as his favourite picture (Millais, 1, pp. 328–30).

The nun or the novice, the soon-to-be 'bride of Christ', is matched by The bridesmaid (14) which Millais reported having completed in January 1851. The subject, on one level, relates to the social ritualisation of marriage which the artist continued to explore through images of single female figures. The bridesmaid must, therefore, be seen in relation to a painting of around 1858 known as The bride or A girl with passion flowers in her hair (M. Warner, 1985, p. 578), Wedding cards: jilted (pre-1855), The violet's message (a half-length figure of a pensive girl removing from an envelope a bunch of violets), The bridesmaid (also known as The lucky slipper) of 1859 (18), Yes or no of 1871 and The bridesmaid of 1879 which portrays the artist's daughter Mary when bridesmaid to her sister, Effie.

The bridesmaid, in Millais's painting of 1851 (14) is 'passing the wedding cake through the ring nine times' (Millais, 1, p. 94). According to custom, this will ensure a vision of her future lover. The subject is, therefore, a variant on the St Agnes' eve story, a fantasy about sexual consummation. The orange blossom at her breast is a symbol of chastity and, as has been pointed out, the silver caster on the table next to the plate containing the cake and the orange is the same as the one used by Millais in Mariana and in the drawing of the nun for the Tennysonian version of St Agnes' eve (M. Warner, The Pre-Raphaelites, no. 37).

At one level the caster is no more than a studio prop that came in handy on more than one occasion. But the common pool from which the ingredients of these secular and religious themes are drawn is worthy of note. The slippage between the nun and the bridesmaid, between the bride of Christ and the bride of man, is not exceptional but intrinsic, underpinning the communication at every level, biographical, thematic, compositional, material, iconographic. The facility with which a caster (unmistakeably phallic in form) can be censer, then sugar-caster, then censer again is startling and suggests shifting boundaries between secular and religious themes and a close tie-up at a symbolic level between the bridesmaid, hopeful of sexual union, Mariana wearily and hopelessly awaiting it, and the nun having abandoned it. Moreover the bridesmaid, with her Magdalene-like pose and her clouds of hair (and hair frequently functions in representation as a form of sexual encoding) (Nead, 1984, p. 34), her figure and expression redolent of the ecstatic sainthood of seventeenth-century Italian painting, personifies an equivalent to the religious ritual in which the novice will participate as she becomes the bride of Christ.

The bridesmaid (14) is a disconcerting painting, not merely on account of the degree of intensely articulated detail concentrated in so small an area and the orange curtains of hair, but also because of its naturalistically rendered detail. This sets up expectations which are then confounded by the symmetry of the composition and by the confusion over the placing of the front picture plane. The subsequent bridesmaid paintings are closer to conventional portrait presentations, but this difference should not cause us to ignore the continuing working out of the theme. The actual means of encoding may differ – thus, for instance, in The bridesmaid of 1859 (18) the woman stands full-length in a garden and the marriage she hopes to make is signified not by a ritual with a ring, but by a lucky slipper and by the explicit male presence in the half-length top-hatted figure of a man who appears behind a parapet watching, unseen by her, as she presents herself to our view. Gardens and walls are, as Casteras has pointed out, a common motif in courtship themes (Casteras, 1986). The sugar-caster and the paraphernalia of rings, oranges and cake are replaced in Yes or no by an ornate and equally phallic silver candlestick and by the letters and photographs signifying the male presence; the thematisation of the not-yet married woman is, however, the same.

The one thing everyone remembers about a bridesmaid is the old adage 'three times a bridesmaid, never a bride'. In depicting bridesmaids Millais establishes a sequence of images of a socially-defined function in which the crucial and momentous boundary between marriage and not-marriage, celibacy and sexuality, woman and girl, is repeatedly invoked. Here the phallic law is at its most powerful; these are not documentary accounts of pathetic 'old maids' having to work for their living, they are depictionss of women defined by the invisible or symbolically present male, the other: father, husband, brother. In narrative terms the theme of phallic authority is displayed in Trust me of 1862 in which a daughter declines to show her father a letter she has received. The bridesmaid is poised between virginity and womanhood, spinsterhood and marriage. In the paintings of bridesmaids, therefore, that phallic authority is manifest symbolically through iconographical detail.

Marriage has always been (at least since the Roman Empire) one of the more prominent occasions of portraiture and one of the events it most commonly celebrates. But it was Sir Joshua Reynolds's *The Montgomery sisters adorning a term of Hymen* that established the narrative of marriage as central to female portraiture in English art. Because marriage is for almost all women of whatever class the only viable means of social valorisation and economic security, the state of the woman prior to marriage was, as de Beauvoir and many historians have acknowledged, particularly contradictory. The state was brittle and insecure because it was, after all, a market economy in which women needed to marry much more than men. But the very forces of that economy created an ideology in which the unmarried woman's state had to be seen to be desirable so that she, too, would seem to need to be persuaded to leave it. Commodities that are readily available lose their value. The before-during-after sequence through which the woman's state was defined by Reynolds leaves no space outside of the concept of marriage for a female identity. The before part of that question, when hypostatised in the figure of the bridesmaid, incorporates both the trajectory towards the ceremony of marriage in which she has participated in a subordinate role *and* the slightly prurient notion of availability construed around one who has, as it were, passed near to the boundary between virginity and sexual intercourse (marriage being legally defined as a ceremony followed by intercourse), but not beyond it.

The wedding ceremony traditionally offers its stage to three women: the mother, the daughter and bride, and the bridesmaid and sister. The bridesmaid is the third woman, the third term in the relationship of the man to his own mother and to that woman who stands in her place as his wife. Through association with the person of the bridesmaid/sister the bride/mother is fixed in her unmarried, virginal state. Of all manifestations of Victorian desire to possess simultaneously the contradictory states of sexual and virginal woman, this is perhaps the most compelling. The erotic undertones of the commonplace arrangement whereby the young sister-in-law, that is, the wife's younger sister, came and lived with the couple and became 'like a real sister, and yet also like a wife' has been identified and discussed by Davidoff and Hall. They draw attention to the passion with which the legal prohibition against marriage to a deceased wife's sister was debated from the 1830s to its abolition in the early twentieth century and suggest that the erotic overtones between brother and sister have an affinity to the pattern observed between father and daughter (p. 351). The ambiguous relationship of the bridesmaid to the marriage at which she is an attendant was, in the Victorian period, given visible expression in the common practice of the bridesmaid/sister accompanying the newly-wed couple on their honeymoon. Holman Hunt married his deceased first wife's younger sister in breach of the law and was compelled to elope to Switzerland to do so; the couple were accompanied by Diana Mulock Craik, the novelist. Her role prior to the nuptials was that of chaperone (Coombs *et al.*, p. 2), but the arrangement also permitted space for the second woman, friend of the bride, within the marriage. Fictional accounts reinforce the currency of the relationship, as for instance in Nicholas Nickleby where Miss Squeers, as bridesmaid, arrives with the honeymoon couple by coach in London four days after the wedding (Ch. 39).

I now wish to return to Millais's drawing The flood (**19**) to which he referred in his letter of January 1851 to Mrs Combe. It was never developed beyond the stage of a drawing but nonetheless fulfilled a major function for the artist as a space in which contradictory and disturbing ideas about marriage could be explored. It is in an important sense the matrix upon which the sequence of drawings of the early 1850s including *A ghost appearing at a wedding ceremony* (**15**) and ultimately the late painting Speak! Speak! (**20**) depend. These menacing and sinister evocations of marriage form a group comparable to that which deals with brides and bridesmaids. By the end of January 1851 Millais had abandoned The flood, at least for the time being whilst The return of the dove to the ark was being painted. This, interestingly, was also known as 'The daughters of Noah' and 'The wives of the sons of Noah', titles which suggest a very particular relationship to the laid-aside Flood drawing (Millais, 1, p. 98). The artist's plans for the latter were set down at length in a further letter to Mrs Combe on 28 May 1851:

I shall endeavour in the picture I have in contemplation – 'For as in the Days that were Before the Flood', etc., etc. – to affect those who may look on it with the awful uncertainty of life and the necessity of always being prepared for death. My intention is to lay the scene at the marriage feast. The bride, elated by her happiness will be playfully showing her wedding-ring to a young girl, who will be in the act of plighting her troth to a man wholly engrossed in his love, the parents of each uniting in congratulation at the consummation of their own and their children's happiness. A drunkard will be railing boisterously at another, less intoxicated, for his cowardice in being somewhat appalled at the view the open window presents . . . In short, all deaf to the prophecy of the Deluge which is swelling before their eyes – all but one figure in their midst, who, upright with closed eyes, prays for mercy for those around her, a patient example of belief standing with, but far from, them placidly awaiting God's will.

I hope, by this great contrast, to excite a reflection on the probable way in which sinners would meet the coming death – all hurrying from height to height as the sea increases; the wretched self-congratulations of the bachelor who, having but himself to save, believes in the prospect of escape; the awful feelings of the husband who sees his wife and children looking in his face for support, and presently disappearing one by one in the pitiless flood as he miserably thinks of his folly in not having taught them to look to God for help in times of trouble . . . One great encouragement to me is the certainty of [the picture] having this one advantage over a sermon, that it will be all at once put before the spectator without that trouble of realisation often lost in the effort of reading or listening. (Millais, 1, pp. 103–5)

Intended as 'a sermon', but one which will save the spectator 'the trouble of realisation often lost in the effort of reading or listening', this allegorical project brings together the anxiety, obligation and fearfulness of marriage as a form of social regulation at a particular historical moment. It does so from the point of view of a man, not that of a woman. Inscribed within the biblical narrative of the Flood – which is, after all, the virtual destruction of the human race and all its social practices – are the institutionalised social rituals of marriage in bourgeois Western society. Later Millais, sorely missing the companionship of his friend Holman Hunt, planned to take this drawing to the Middle East with him and join Hunt. He described it as work 'which I shall be able to paint anywhere and take about with me' (The Pre-Raphaelites, no. 171). The flood possessed the status of a talisman for Millais, an exceptional form of personal allegory which he associated with his keenest, and possibly homosexual, feelings. All Millais's work of this period is strongly characterised by its identification with particular locations and detailed 'truth to nature' studies. The flood is in a category of its own, a work one can take anywhere.

There is no doubt that in market terms, The flood (19) would not have been a very saleable painting. Nonetheless, a further reason why it was never finished may well have been because it simply became redundant. The happiness of the bride in the shadow of disaster, the complacent oblivion of the parents and the sinister side of this central heterosexual celebration of bourgeois family life are relentlessly exposed in the series of Hogarthian drawings already discussed: Married for money (16), A ghost appearing at a wedding ceremony (15), and others. The presence of death in the context of love and marriage is the subject, furthermore, of Speak! Speak! (20) and of the drawing The dying man in which the ghastly presence of the skeletal figure dominates that most powerful of all domestic settings, the fireside. In his most speculative late essay, Beyond the pleasure principle, Freud suggested that 'the pleasure principle seems actually to serve the death instincts' (Freud, 11, p. 338); the powerful connection between sex and death in these images thus may be seen not only to have particular historical resonances given social practice, legislation and dominant bourgeois ideology, but also to carry profound implications for the formation in representation of sexual identity.

These correspondences are paralleled in other drawings: the playful showing of the wedding ring to the young girl in The flood (**19**) is taken up in The bridesmaid (**14**) and the drunkard and the vain woman are types who reappear in another drawing in the series, The race meeting. All these works are executed in a graphic documentary style connotative of immediacy and public debate. They suggest, therefore, something akin to a series of magazine illustrations, a sequence of familiar types, linked by a narrative of disaster. Looked at as a whole, however, the group can be seen as specific illustrative instances, each one relating back to the allegorical matrix. It is not, therefore, a question of whether Millais was making documentary images or symbolic paintings. Nor is it a question of whether or not one or other image can be perceived in relation to the artist's own history. Here is a declaration on the part of the artist, a declaration both verbal and visual. The flood proposes a series of human types; each one is defined by reference to two events that have equal value in the narrative (as verbally conveyed) and in the image. One is the marriage celebration and the other is the flood. The organisation of the field of vision in The flood reinforces that equivalence, for outside is the flood and inside is the marriage. Between the symmetrical curve of the table's edge and the rectangular opening of the small shuttered window, these human types play out their futile but inevitable roles.

The idea of a 'sermon' which Millais so substantially articulated in his letter about The flood touches upon the role of the verbal narrative in these works. We began with the sermon of the marriage service, the textual underpinning of Millais's marriage-related themes. In the last work in which the idea of marriage plays a part, Speak! Speak! (**20**) painted at the very end of Millais's long career, the bride is explicitly connected with disaster. Here the wedding and the Flood are again conjoined. But this time it is in the context not of a sermon in paint but of a thematisation of lack of speech. This desperate wordlessness, a communication beyond the grave, is the silent articulation of the ultimate desire, the anticipation of death.

Notes

I would like to acknowledge Alastair Grieve, who first raised the question of marriage in relation to Millais, and thank Malcolm Warner and Robert Twyman-Heaven for their advice, Gabriel Naughton and Leslie Parris for help with illustrations and John Barrell and Joany

Hichberger for reading and commenting on this chapter in draft.

1 For details of images by Millais see the list of titles and locations at the end of this chapter.
2 See, for example, the organisation of Malcolm Warner's authoritative catalogue of Millais's
   work, *The professional career of John Everett Millais to 1863*, PhD, University of London, Courtauld
   Institute of Art, 1985.
3 MS. Huntington Library, San Marino, California, HH 385 and 387, quoted by M. Warner,
   p. 96, to whom I am grateful for permission to quote.
4 Grieve, 1976, p. 26, first raises this question and draws attention to Millais's friendship with
   Coventry Patmore.
5 The painting was in English collections until 1935.
6 A photograph in the Witt Library of a painting (Viscount Leverhulme, c. 1860) showing a
   young, bare-headed novice fastening her robe, a work of almost the same dimensions as
   The bridesmaid, might seem to be a candidate but is, according to Warner, by Collinson, not
   Millais.
7 For a detailed account of the iconography of the nun in Millais's work and its relationship
   to the events of his own life see E. Shefer, 'The nun and the convent in Pre-Raphaelite art',
   The journal of Pre-Raphaelite studies, 6: 2, May 1986, pp. 70–6.

Works by J. E. Millais cited in text, listed in order of mention

Stitch! Stitch!, 1876, G. F. Watts collection, present location unknown, engraving Witt Library,
   London
Virtue and vice, 1853, drawing, private collection, reproduced Grieve, 1976, no. 9
Lorenzo and Isabella, 1849, National Museums and Galleries on Merseyside
The Benjamites seizing their brides, 1840, oil on canvas, location unknown, reproduced, Millais, 1,
   p. 23
The proposal, c. 1840, Sheffield City Art Galleries
Cymon and Iphigenia, 1848, oil on canvas, the Rt. Hon. Viscount Leverhulme, reproduced *The
   Pre-Raphaelites*, no. 10
The woodman's daughter, 1851, oil on canvas, Guildhall Art Gallery, Corporation of London
The order of release, 1746, 1852–53, oil on canvas, Tate Gallery
The bride (girl with passion flowers in her hair), c. 1858, oil on panel, Trustees of the late Sir Kenneth
   Clark
The gambler's wife, 1869, location unknown, photo Witt Library, London
Wedding cards: jilted, pre-1855, location unknown, photo Witt Library, London
Mariana, 1850–1, oil on panel, Makins collection, reproduced *The Pre-Raphaelites*, no. 35
Ophelia, 1852, oil on canvas, *Tate Gallery*
The vale of rest, 1858, oil on canvas, Tate Gallery, London
*A Huguenot, on St. Bartholomew's day refusing to shield himself from danger by wearing the Roman Catholic
   badge*, 1851–2, oil on canvas, Makins collection, reproduced *The Pre-Raphaelites*, no. 41
Autumn leaves, 1855–6, oil on canvas, City of Manchester Art Galleries
Spring (apple blossom), 1859, oil on canvas, the Rt. Hon. Viscount Leverhulme, reproduced *The
   Pre-Raphaelites*, no. 96
Married for money, 1853, drawing, private collection, reproduced *The Pre-Raphaelites*, no. 188
A ghost appearing at a wedding ceremony, 1853–4, drawing, Victoria and Albert Museum
Speak! Speak!, 1895, oil on canvas, Tate Gallery
Peace concluded, 1856, oil on canvas, Sotheby's 3 April 1968 (105)
The flood (the eve of the deluge), 1850, drawing, British Museum
The bridesmaid, 1851, oil on panel, Fitzwilliam Museum, Cambridge

The nun, unlocated, details unknown

The eve of St. Agnes, 1862–3, oil on canvas, H.M. Queen Elizabeth the Queen Mother, reproduced The Pre-Raphaelites, no. 122

St. Agnes's eve, 1854, drawing, private collection, reproduced The Pre-Raphaelites, no. 200

The violet's message, c. 1853, oil on panal, Lady Lever Gallery, Port Sunlight

The bridesmaid, 1859, oil on canvas, location unknown, reproduced Apollo, front cover, Feb. 1948

Yes or no, 1871, oil on canvas, location unknown, photo Witt Library, London

The bridesmaid, 1879, oil on canvas, location unknown, photo Witt Library, London

The return of the dove to the ark, 1851, oil on canvas, Ashmolean Museum, Oxford

Trust me, 1862, oil on canvas, Forbes Magazine Collection

The dying man, 1853–54, pen and sepia ink with wash, Yale Center for British Art

The race meeting, 1853, pen and black ink, Ashmolean Museum, Oxford

7

Fantasy and arrested desire in Edward Burne-Jones's Briar-Rose series
Larry D. Lutchmansingh

Sir Edward Burne-Jones (1833–98) defied his age with the declaration, 'the more materialistic Science becomes, the more angels shall I paint', and claimed to feel 'not so much as if I belonged to another time or country but to another planet altogether', to 'love the immaterial', to 'wish for ancient times – sigh heavily for them', and to 'hate this world, (to) want it to end'.[1] Yet he had earlier acquired a certain political notoriety, being described by William Allingham in 1866 as a 'People's Man', by Charles Eliot Norton in 1869 as 'a strong, almost a bitter Republican', to whom 'the condition of England is . . . a scandal and a reproach', and having on his own part hailed the French republic in 1870.[2] But none of this political concern is evoked in Burne-Jones's vast artistic production. On the contrary, ever since Dante Gabriel Rossetti called him 'one of the nicest young fellows in – *Dreamland*', his art has been characterised in terms of reverie, fantasy, and a highly privatised imagination.[3] Hence the typical judgements of the artist's works, that, according to Lord David Cecil, 'whatever their title, they are pictures of Burne-Jones's private daydream; visions of the never-never land he had created for his own delight', so that 'he is fully convincing only when a fairy tale is actually his subject'; or that the tendency of the work 'is to dwell always in a world of dreams, to eschew everything that comes too close to merely human and everyday interest, and keeps us in the region of mild, semi-religious mysticism' (Cecil, p. 145, p. 150; Spalding, p. 16).

These qualities of the work and the record of his own positions and opinions suggest a complex tension, and a deep-seated ambivalence, in Burne-Jones's consciousness and creative impulse. The alternation in his life of submission to, and defiance against, an unbearable historical fate, of utopian flights and insight into political reality, and of high moral purpose alongside failures of will, have not been sufficiently probed.

Instead, we have had a rather one-dimensional picture of an ineffectual and escapist dreamer, and of an art entirely given to fantasy and dissociated imagination. Nor has the frequency of appeal to these qualities of the work and the consciousness been matched by any interest in their precise nature or etiology. One reason for this may be the simple and unexamined prejudice about artists in general, but about this one in particular, that matters of the lived experience do not meaningfully impinge upon creative expression, that, in the words of Lord Cecil, 'his art was the expression of his inner life which pursued its own way, unconnected with his outer life and unaffected by its events, so that it becomes impossible to fuse the two lives into a single tale' (p. 124). Yet Burne-Jones's claim that 'imagination doesn't end with my work: I go on always in that strange land that is more true and real', and his desire 'to forget the world and be inside a picture', intimated not simply a dissociation of sensibility, but a troubled simultaneity in which a crushing and inescapable social reality cast its shadow over all productive activity (*Memorials*, 1, p. 116, and 2, p. 305).

If we accept that Burne-Jones 'is fully convincing only when a fairy tale is actually his subject' with these disjunctions of consciousness in mind, we may come closer to an understanding of the workings of his productive powers, and of the ways in which the contradictions of his actual experience necessarily mediate and shape his art. For the adoption of the fairy tale, myth, and legend that figure so commonly in his work must itself have been the occasion of a contest of faculties and allegiances. This would be apparent in the role with which Ruskin invested Burne-Jones, that of 'the modern painter of mythology', who had to give imaginative form to 'the visions described by the wisest of men (of the past) as embodying their most pious thoughts and their most exalted doctrines . . . bringing the resources of accomplished art to unveil the hidden splendour of old imagination (Ruskin, 33, p. 296). But it would particularly be the case in the several instances of Burne-Jones's adaptation of subjects from fantasy and fairy-tale (e.g. 'Beauty and the beast', 'Cinderella', and 'Sleeping beauty').

Ruskin's conception of the purpose of 'mythic' painting concerned the representation of 'only general truths, or abstract ideas' (Ruskin, 33, p. 293). An alternative view of such forms of artistic production posits, however, the genre of fairy-tale as imbricated in social and political particulars, that genre offering a paradigm of the material oppression of which it is the obverse. If we adopt this model we see Burne-Jones confronting in the fairy-tale the very ruses whereby fantasy and imagination, in a symbolic mode, create a sense of enchantment as the medium of an emancipatory potential, and generate the utopian hope of recovering the unities lost in the process of rationalist fragmentation and reconstruction of the subject under capitalism. For such a utopian impulse is a 'critique of what is present' (Bloch), a 'determined negation of that which merely is' (Adorno) in the regime of capital. Acquiring as it does, according to Frederic Jameson, a 'semi-autonomous coherence', it becomes able to 'compensate for the dehumanization of experience reification brings with it, and to rectify the otherwise intolerable effects of the new process'.[4]

Burne-Jones's negotiation of these issues, and a symptomatic historical representation of some of the internal crises of both the later phase of Pre-Raphaelitism with which he is associated, as well as late nineteenth-century British art in general, are to be observed in his extended treatment of the 'Sleeping Beauty' story.[5] Between 1870 and 1895 he worked on three separate series based on the story whose folk origin is buried in the distant past, but which was popularised by Charles Perrault as 'La Belle au bois dormant' in his Histoire ou contes de temps passé of 1697 (first translated into English in Robert Sambler's Histories or tales of past times of 1729), and by the brothers Grimm in Kinder-und Haus-Marchen (translated into English by Edgar Taylor in German popular stories in 1823). In addition, he had illustrated the story in a series of nine ceramic tiles in 1863. In the first (1870–73) and third (1872–95) of the Briar-Rose series, the artist chose to present the story in three narrative sequences which offered rich pictorial possibilities. He repeated these in the second series (1870–90) in panels titled The prince enters the briar wood (21), The council chamber, and The sleeping beauty (22), and he added a fourth panel between the second and third, titled The rose bower. This series was exhibited to much acclaim in Agnew's in 1890, the reviewer in the Magazine of art, for example, calling them 'epoch-making pictures', which 'for some qualities are equal to anything that has ever been done since painting began' (13 June 1890, xxxiv).

A singular problem of interpretation is presented by the absence in all three series of a scene depicting the consummating moment of the prince's embrace of the sleeping princess, which would awaken her and all the court and bring about the resumption of history after the hundred-year respite. The scene is described as follows in the Grimms' 'Little Briar Rose':

There she lay, so beautiful that he could not turn his eyes away; and he stooped down and gave her a kiss. But as soon as he kissed her, Briar-rose opened her eyes and awoke, and looked at him quite sweetly. Then they went down together, and the King awoke, and the Queen, and the whole court, and looked at each other in great astonishment. And the horses in the courtyard stood up and shook them-selves; the hounds jumped up and wagged their tails; the pigeons upon the roof pulled out their heads from under their wings, looked round, and flew into the open country; the flies on the wall crept again; the fire in the kitchen burned up and flickered and cooked the meat; the joint began to turn and sizzle again, and the cook gave the boy such a box on the ear that he screamed, and the maid finished plucking the fowl. (Brackert and Sander, pp. 121–2)

Burne-Jones would also have been familiar with the corresponding scene in 'The day-dream,' Tennyson's 1842 treatment of the story:

A touch, a kiss! the charm was snapt.
    There rose a noise of striking clocks,
And feet that ran, and doors that clapt,
    And barking dogs, and crowing cocks;
A fuller light illumined all,
    A breeze thro' all the garden swept,
A sudden hubbub shook the hall,
    And sixty feet the fountain leapt.

A striking metaphor in the following stanza captures the resuscitated energies of the court:

And all the long-pent stream of life
    Dash'd downward in a cataract.
(Tennyson, p. 99)

Burne-Jones would not permit this sense of suddenly resumed activity, so dramatically focused in the narrative structure of the accounts at hand, to disturb the almost complete stasis of his own version, with its frieze-like panorama of figures uncannily frozen in a perpetual sleep that cannot easily be distinguished from death itself. One reviewer thought the tapestry-like design, 'everything being in simple planes, by which means a certain quaint formality is obtained ... fits most admirably Perrault's fairy legend' (*Magazine of art*, June 1890, xxxiv). But Burne-Jones's refusal to have the bewitchment of the court undone makes of his treatment of the story in the series, taken as a narrative whole, a curiou-sly eccentric one, demanding some explanation. Our perplexity is increased by the incongruity of the two recorded explanations given by the artist. His own words invoke the psychological transaction between himself and the viewers of his paintings: 'I want it to stop with the Princess asleep and to tell no more,' he said, 'to leave all the afterwards to the invention and imagination of people, and tell them no more' (*Memo-rials*, 2, p. 195). The manoeuvre of concealment as a means of engaging

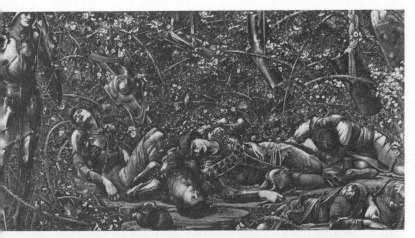

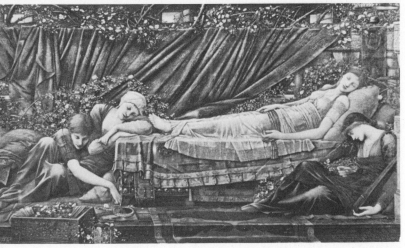

E. Burne-Jones, The second Briar-Rose series: **21** 1, *The prince enters the briar wood;*
22 4, *The sleeping beauty*

the audience's own emanicipatory vision may involve a radical utopian impulse. But this promise needs to be seen in the contradicting light of the more pragmatic reason which the artist apparently conveyed to Lady Burne-Jones, who wrote that 'he said that such a final picture must have been a dramatic one, and would not have fitted the lyrical quiet and romance of the other four' (*Memorials*, 2, p. 195). The issue then becomes one of the artist's apparent choice to convert the dramatic element of the narrative to quiescent poetical ends. The choice suggests to Harrison and Waters, authors of a major monograph on the artist, 'an indication of his pre-occupation with the theme of sleep, a preoccupation which relates to his own withdrawal from contemporary problems' (pp. 151, 153). But this only begs the crucial question. For, as so often in his creative career (and as this discussion will attempt to establish), the peculiar languor and passivity of Burne-Jones's figures register not only an implacable mental force in the artist, but also a systematic repression of the active principle, and it is this that calls for specific analysis. When Burne-Jones opted to add a fourth panel to the series, he illustrated not the breaking of the magic spell, but a subdued scene of six sleeping female workers, which certainly reinforces the 'lyrical quiet and romance' of the whole series, but adds little to the dramatic unfolding of the narrative and deprives it of the recuperative closure of the original story.

The treatment of the scene of awakening and fulfilment would have required either the appearance of the liberator prince in two separate places, or his transference from the first to the last (or additional) panel. Although Burne-Jones could have conceived the first alternative as disturbing the narrative unity of the series, as he had envisaged it, with the prince appearing in two separate places, this is not the reason given by him. On the other hand, it should have been fully acceptable in a series envisaged as representation of fantasy. Indeed, he had already adopted such an arrangement in his decorative treatment of the story in a set of nine ceramic tiles in 1863 (now in the Victoria and Albert Museum). That the artist may have skirted the second alternative is suggested in two preparatory studies for the first panel, in neither of which the prince appears. (One of these is reproduced (**23**)). Indeed, the disposition of the reclining figure at the far left of both of these studies suggests a structural completeness, to which the figure of the prince adds a perhaps artificial accent. Moreover, Burne-Jones appears to have been somewhat undecided about the physical disposition, dramatic action, and expressive function of the prince. In the first *Briar-Rose* series, the prince had been placed gazing resolutely in the direction of his forward movement, his

shield athwart and his sword drawn to cut his way through the over-
grown rose-bush (**24**). In the second series, in contrast, he stands apart,
his legs ambiguously suggestive of both hesitation and imminent action,
his rueful gaze directed to a distant point, his sword held impassively at
his side, and his shield held as if to shut off the view of his defeated
forerunners (**21**). This figure hardly fits the heroic role into which
William Morris cast him in the stanzas which he penned to accompany
Burne-Jones's painting:

> Here lies the hoarded love, the key
> To all the treasure that shall be;
> Come fated hand the gift to take,
> And smite this sleeping world awake.
> (Morris, 1911, 9, p. 190)

This indecisive and incongruous aspect of the figure of the prince did
strike at least one contemporary critic, who asked,

> Is this dainty warrior the long-expected deliverer whose coming is to 'smite the
> sleeping world awake'? He pushes away the branches with his shield, and
> actually holds a drawn sword in his hand; but is there really and truly a fighting-
> man within that choice and beautifully polished amours, borrowed for the
> occasion from a *bijou* collection?
> (Shaw-Sparrow, p. 20)

Burne-Jones's apparent difficulties in treating the fairy-tale of the
'Sleeping beauty' need to be seen in the broader perspective of the
critical changes which the genre as such was undergoing in the nineteenth century. On the one hand, there was the intrinsic problem of
using 'allegorical forms to make a statement about Christian goodness in
contrast to the greed and materialism' of the age (Zipes, 1987, xx). On the
other, there was a tendency among some writers to suppress the popular, radical, and magical impulses of the fairy-tale in the ideological
interest of dominant bourgeois values. In 1866, for example, at roughly
the mid-point between Burne-Jones's straightforward depiction of the
prince bestowing the magical kiss upon the sleeping princess in the sixth
of his series of nine ceramic tiles, and 1870, when he began his first
painting series on the theme (and which, as we have observed, lacks that
final scene), the *Cornhill magazine* published an adaption of the 'sleeping
beauty' story. But in this instance the prototypes of the original story are
attached to a landowning family that appears to have come down in the
world, whose everyday life is marked by idleness, boredom, and
puritanical restraint, and whose only transaction with the outside world
takes the form of the contesting of property claims with relatives. Cecilia
Lulworth of Lulworth Hall, in the princess role, 'never thought of anything but the utterest commonplaces and platitudes', and 'considered

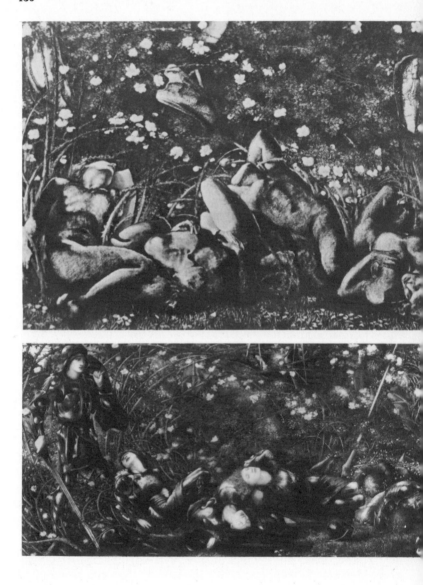

E. Burne-Jones: **23** *The sleeping knights;* **24** The first Briar-Rose series, 1, *The prince enters the wood*

that being respectable and decorous, and a little pompous and overbearing, was the duty of every well-brought up lady and gentleman'.[6] Frank Lulworth, her cousin, in the role of the prince, is invited over to 'talk business matters,' and they fall in love (p. 563). This unbearably prosaic adaptation of the fairy-tale in effect discounts those qualities of magic, fantasy, and enigma which have traditionally constituted the means of its appeal and subliminal reassurance, and it thereby neutralises its radical emancipatory potential.

Although Burne-Jones, on his part, does effectively impart to his series of paintings an aura of fantasy and enchantment, his failure (or refusal) to represent the moment of recuperation in effect has the same inhibitive result. Indeed, it suggests precisely that his legendary power of evoking worlds of dream and enchantment in painting could not sustain the promise of renewal and deliverance that was central to the tradition of the fairy-tale. There is, therefore, a special poignancy in his equation of a painting with 'a beautiful romantic dream of something that never was, never will be – in light better than any light that ever shone – in a land no-one can define, or remember, only desire' (quoted in Wood, p. 119). One needs to interrogate this curious and abstract formulation of desire, whose coupling with the impossibility of memory becomes matched in the paintings of the 'sleeping beauty' story by the operation of desire without the possibility of prevision or hope of fulfilment. The effect of this upon his representation of the fairy-tale is that desire cannot complete its expected and self-fulfilling course of development. For the fairy-tale, as Max Lüthi writes in his essay on 'sleeping beauty', 'fills its hearers with confidence that a new, larger life is to come after the deathlike sleep . . . a new form of contact and community will follow' (p. 24), the deathlike sleep also possibly referring to the loss of a 'golden age of humanity – and of childhood', to be recovered at a later and higher level of existence.[7] It is necessary, however, to recognise in the genre 'the social function of a literary genre that originally belonged to the lower classes and reflected their dreams of emancipation, their optimism, their longing for an end to the oppression of person and class'.[8] Not only would these possibilities be curtailed by Burne-Jones's treatment of the 'sleeping beauty' story: if, according to Robert Darnton, 'in most of the tales wish fulfillment turns into a program for survival, not a fantasy of escape', he would appear to reverse the very terms upon which the narrative completes its dynamic of utopian reassurance (Darnton, p. 44).

For the dissociation of these forward-looking functions from fantasy and imagination is what we observe in the *Briar-Rose* series, and the particular significance of this is that his art can no longer speak to the condition of persons but must instead remain tied to the individual utterance. But this is often an utterance of desperation. At the very time when he needed completion of the great second series of paintings, he mused, 'how nice it would be to live five hundred years, taking less and less part in the world but watching it with big eyes' (*Memorials*, 2, p. 201) which can be taken as an apposite gloss upon the works themselves, representing as they do an immense hiatus of life and activity, graphically observed, but without the possibility of redeeming action. Burne-Jones was personally shaped by historical forces, and himself perceived the course of history in such a way as to experience an overwhelming world-weariness and paralysis of the will to action. The Birmingham of his early years revealed the noxious and dehumanising effects of industrialisation at their nightmarish worst, at the time when one of its entrepreneurs, Joseph Chamberlain, was about 'to produce twice as many steel screws as the whole of the rest of Britain', Burne-Jones was discovering Malory's *Morte d'Arthur* (Fitzgerald, p. 37).

The Birmingham Chartist riots of 1839 saw his father being drafted as a special constable, and the child 'suffered many things in imagination because a maid-servant . . . used to fan his terrors by grisly stories of what was happening, or might happen, in the streets' (*Memorials*, 1, pp. 9–10). As so often in the middle-class Victorian household, the maidservant both signified the underclass and served as a means of instilling a fasci-nated terror of that little-known world in the child (see Stallybrass and White, Ch. 4). Lady Burne-Jones detected a connection between this experience and the troubled sleep and bad dreams of his entire childhood, and indeed concluded that, as a result, 'all through his life he was a dreamer of dreams by night as well as by day' (*Memorials*, 1, p. 10).

The life-long pattern of Burne-Jones's recoil from social reality and escape into a world of dream and fantasy, then, had a specific historical and biographical determination. The prevalence of subjects from myth, legend and fairy-tale in his art, and indeed, the general revival of interest in such subjects in his lifetime after a long period of neglect, need to be understood in terms of the wider historical pattern of growing alienation, as in the individual instance of Burne-Jones, from an oppress-ive and unfathomable social reality (Zipes, 1987, p. xv). But in thus returning to a repressed fantasy tradition, the question arises about the capacity of an already assailed and troubled consciousness to sustain its utopian force. The issue emerges with a particular saliency in an artist such as Burne-Jones, the essential character and power of whose work are taken to lie in its mythical and visionary aspect. That the engagement was to be deeply straining and self-divisive was signalled by one of his early drawings, an 'allegorical' self-portrait, described as follows by Lady Burne-Jones:

It shews the figure of a man seated in mournful dejection before a desk where lies an unfinished drawing of an angel. A small broken statue of an angel also lies at his feet. The man's eyes are closed, and his head rests wearily upon one hand, while in the other he holds an hour-glass from which but few of the sands have run. The background is of heavy rain falling into a dark sea, and underneath it is written, 'When shall I arise and the night be gone?' (*Memorials*, 1, p. 103)

The curious drawing described here represents the ominous interruption of the artist's creative activity; his apparent sleep, his unfinished image of the angel, and the hour-glass in his hand suggest an analogue – earlier in time and in a personal, private register – of some of those features of the *Briar-Rose* series that we have noted as representative. In those paintings too, activity has come to a standstill under the magic spell that hangs over all; the hour-glass that signals the relentless passage of time reappears at the side of the sleeping king on the right of *The council chamber* from the second series, a thematic effect reinforced by a sun-dial in *The garden court* panel from the third series (City Art Gallery, Bristol); the 'night' of the drawing is extended into the interminable sleep of the court; and the cessation of work is represented in *The garden court*, whose composition is bisected by a vertical post, with three weavers on the right immobilised at their loom, and three maids at the left likewise immobilised at the fountain where they were about to draw three pitchers of water. But most striking of all is the intimation of inexplicable forces which grip and constrain the work of the depicted artist of the allegorical drawing and the prince of the first panel. The incapacitation of the will to move from the thought to the necessary act in both figures designates the very condition of Burne-Jones himself, who would not represent in the paintings the expected progress from long, deathlike sleep to renewed life and activity.

Since his years at Oxford, when he projected the formation of a brotherhood to wage 'Holy Warfare against the age', Burne-Jones had denounced what he perceived as the utilitarianism, materialism, and increasing barbarism of his times, especially as they appeared to thwart the artist. He was, therefore, frequently nostalgic for ancient and medieval times, and is remembered as wishing himself, 'not an Englishman of today, but a Florentine of the fourteenth century', a vain attempt, it would seem, to stem the attrition of living memory, and to fill the void of present identity, by recourse to the plenitude of an idealised past.[9] His fellow-artist, Fernand Khnopff, perceptively connected Burne-Jones's fixation upon the past and horror of the present (although gratuitously dramatising the experience of injury):

Yes, a fifteenth-century Italian; but with the added inheritance of suffering and moral distressfulness which falls to the sad lot of the men of the nineteenth century – haunted by the same ideal as pursues us all, and the craving even to bleed in the clutch of Chimaera, if only so we may escape through dreams from the horrors of reality. (p. 525)

What Burne-Jones thought particularly enviable about the medieval and early renaissance artist was that he worked in a public sphere and in a shared idiom, in other words, in a context of what his friend and professional collaborator, William Morris, called 'popular art'.[10] Among his uncompleted projects was a series conceived in such terms and representing the 'whole history of the world' in four ages of mankind (Memorials, 1, 308–9). But like Morris, he realised that the irresistible force of nineteenth-century commodification had undermined the social pre-conditions of such an art. Asserting (around 1874) that 'a good artist ought to work for public purposes', and that 'no private person ought to own pictures', he lamented, 'I'm as much a slave kept in Leyland's back parlour as a Greek artist at the time of the Empire. Desperate harm it was to keep such artists spending all their talent in the cutting of minute gems that should have been used in statues and great pictures' (Lago, p. 179).

The reference is to Frederick Leyland (1831–92) of Liverpool, a wealthy, self-made shipping magnate, whose patronage of artists was as generous as it was problematic for them. He it was who provoked the even more bitter complaint from Dante Gabriel Rossetti in 1873: 'I have often said that to be an artist is just the same thing as to be a whore, as far as dependence on the whims and fancies of individuals is concerned' (D. G. Rossetti, 1967, p. 1175). The relationship between Leyland and Rossetti reveals some of the most excruciating elements of late nineteenth-century art patronage. Their correspondence shows the artist frequently reduced to importuning and wheedling the patron, even to the point, for example, of writing to him about a painting in hand that 'it will be one of my cheapest at 120 gs.', and a duplicity of conduct is indicated in his confiding to a friend about a Leyland commission, 'I have accepted a distasteful but temptingly lucrative offer to make a replica . . . a very lazy leisurely job which can be done at odd times' (The Rossetti-Leyland letters, p. 101). On his part, Leyland was interested primarily in luxurious representations of women from poetry and legend, to be used as 'furnishings of my house', and he betrayed an unusual concern with the sizes of paintings and their depicted figures, which he held to be 'an important consideration when pictures are merely used for rooms and not in a gallery', that is, in a private as distinct from a public context (pp. 16, 25). Rossetti chafed at these conditions, and he put his impatience on record in connection with another patron of similar taste (*The owl and the Rossettis*, no. 343).

Burne-Jones must have felt similarly, but his complaints were less freely or indignantly expressed. The figures of the 'slave' and the 'prostitute', employed with such seeming casualness by the two artists to convey the nature of their relationship to the same patron, signify some complex changes in nineteenth-century artistic culture as well as in the artists' subjective experience of those changes. The whore, wrote Walter Benjamin, is 'seller and commodity in one' (Benjamin, p. 171). The metaphors define art and artist in terms not of creative, inspired, and necessary work for a known and sympathetic public, but rather of mere production at the behest of powerful, private, and arbitrary forces. That the relationship between artist and patron was 'rooted in a power both men understood very well, the power of money,' would have evoked in Burne-Jones's mind a sense of the sheer historical distance of the apparently more conducive milieu of the medieval artist (*The Rossetti-Leyland letters*, p. xvii).

Conversely, the images of prostitute and slave begin to define the modern art-collector. They suggest that the collector, in the person of Leyland, is one who redirects to art-objects the same dynamic of expropriation as he does to the commodities of trade. It is not surprising that Leyland was concerned to extract, in a literal sense, the maximum value from the yardage of drawings and paintings. In the process, what we might call, following Marx, the use-value of art, is usurped by an exchange-value, and it is the former entity, now repressed, that Burne-Jones rhetorically equates with the social and productive aspect of medieval and early Renaissance art. The confusion experienced by the artists and their despairing responses register the insidious tendency in art production and patronage whose general character in the wider economic and social sphere was initially sketched by Marx as one of commodification. In the commodity system, accordingly, labour is experienced not as a vital social process but as the objective property of its products, and social relations assume 'the fantastic form of a relation between things' (Marx, p. 165). This is a systematic abstraction which, according to Jean Baudrillard, both arises with the generalisation of exchange value and negates the very 'contradictions spawned by the process of real labour' (Baudrillard, p. 92). From somewhat different angles, Baudrillard and, earlier Benjamin, explained how this development was mirrored in the experience of the collector. For Benjamin, the collector within the commodity system became an inhabitant of the interior, the place of refuge of art:

He made the glorification of things his concern. To him fell the task of Sisyphus which consisted of stripping things of their commodity character by means of his possession of them. But he conferred upon them only a fancier's value, rather than use-value. The collector dreamed that he was in a world which was not only far-off in distance and in time, but which was also a better one, in which to be sure people were just as poorly provided with what they needed as in the world of everyday, but in which things were free from the bondage of being useful. (Benjamin, pp. 168–9)

This 'fancier's value' corresponds, in Baudrillard's analysis, to the completeness of the abstraction and 'total artificiality of the sign' which serve to 'deny the reality of castration' in the modern collector, and, in compensation, to 'weave around himself a closed and invulnerable world that dissolves all obstacles to the realization of desire' (Baudrillard, p. 93). These characterisations of the collector point to the futility – and the immense irony – of the very accomplice of the commodification process seeking a realm of decommodified values in works of art. For the commodity system works precisely to negate 'the physical nature of the commodity and the material [dinglich] relations arising out of this' (Marx, p. 165), making the object merely a 'sign object . . . eviscerated of its substance and history, and reduced to the state of marking a difference, epitomizing a whole system of differences' (Baudrillard, p. 93). This explains the occlusion of those putatively authentic qualities which Burne-Jones would find in the art of the past, that is, before commodification and what he perceives as the evil of private appropriation.

Reacting against the chaos of this development, fantasy, according to Benjamin, is turned 'back upon the primal past', for 'in the dream in which every epoch sees in images the epoch which is to succeed it, the latter appears with elements of prehistory' (Benjamin, p. 159). This may explain another dimension of Burne-Jones's nostalgia for the world of the fourteenth-century Florentine artist. Yet he is incapable of giving concrete expression to the forward-looking half of Benjamin's utopian formula, that is, to the succeeding moment of fulfilment that complements the retrospective vision. That would require precisely the kind of self-mediating creative process that is undermined by experience of the abstraction of artistic work under the regime of commodification. The sensuous and vital fulfilment afforded by that particular power of imagination is what the artist must now renounce. For, according to Peter Leonard, the transformation of useful goods into commodities creates, 'at the psychological level, an exchange value consciousness, where the human being becomes indifferent to or unaware of the original use-value of that which he or she produces' (Leonard, p. 57; Schneider, pp. 121–9). Furthermore, 'this psychological transformation in the individual in commodity production involves *instinctual renunciation* in so far as the individual's "needs" become relatively detached from concrete sensuous satisfactions and become, instead, attached to . . . *abstract* satisfactions, namely money' (Leonard, p. 57). Burne-Jones's personal translation of this process is expressed in his 'great complaint . . . that a workman could not turn out honest work that would last', in his painful knowledge that although he was 'engaged in producing', he was misused and frustrated in his work, and in his poignant regret over the absence of a community of like-minded artists, which made him feel 'a great sense of loneliness . . . as if no other artist wanted the same things at all, and as if I must be wrong'.[11]

Both the enforced renunciation of artistic gratification as well as the difficulty of imaginatively envisioning the end of such renunciation inform Burne-Jones's allegorical self-portrait and the *Briar-Rose* paintings. The psychodynamic force which, for example, inhibits representation of the climactic narrative and symbolic moment of the 'sleeping beauty' story – the moment that projects its own principle of self-realising gratification – functions at a more encompassing level of the artist's creativity to mystify the sphere of public life and activity while magnifying the private sphere of dream and desire. In psychological terms, this splitting of the subject requires that the ego must continually adjust itself to the abstract and rationalised modes of a commodity system, while instinctual nature is banished to the private sphere of the id. In this situation, the very conditions of the gratification of desire are undermined, so that desire itself is foregrounded and problematised. Unrealisable in the present moment of abstract and commodified experience, desire is retrospectively fixated either upon the primal happiness and pre-Oedipal gratification of childhood, or upon the imagined virtues of some bygone age, both of which were presumably marked by the beneficent influence of use-values.

Just such a redemptive vision was inspired in the minds of some beholders of Burne-Jones's second *Briar-Rose* series, one of whom claimed to see in them a link with the 'primal', the 'unremembered ages, when mental contact with the outer world was closer, the nervous connection with phenomena more intimate, when vision was almost tactile' (Wilson, p. 172). In the last painting of the series, *The Sleeping Beauty*, (**22**) such a regression is hinted at in the deathlike sleep of the princess and her attendants, reinforced by the suggestion of a tomb-sculpture in the reclining figure of the former. At a more personal level, the artist's own childhood and the mother he never knew are evoked by the symbolic reference to the immaculate conception in the banner of the Virgin with crescent moon that hangs behind and above the princess: the princess who will never be awakened also figuring as the mother whom the artist was never to know (for she had died a week after his birth), and in the painting of whom Burne-Jones recorded having experienced an unusual depression (*Memorials*, 2, p. 164). As in the projection of a future, so even in the evocation of childhood gratification, there is an insinuation of incompleteness.

This marks a point of overdetermination where elements of personal history and social experience are interfused in a paralysis of creative activity and a sense of abjection. Adorno has suggested that utopia, as a symbolic restoration of the unity lost in the process of capitalist abstraction, and death, are mutually exclusive, so that it becomes impossible for the artist to evoke a utopian consummation without at the same time banishing death (Bloch, p. 10). The impossibility of such a move is what we witness in Burne-Jones's *Briar Rose* series, where the deathlike sleep of the princess registers precisely the fragmentation of the psyche and the frustration of desire in the era of the commodity.

Notes

1 Burne-Jones in Buckley, p. 164; *Burne-Jones talking* . . ., pp. 72, 93, 181. See also *Memorials of Edward Burne-Jones* . . ., 1, pp. 84, 140; 2, pp. 17, 84, 97–8.
2 Allingham, p. 139; *Letters of Charles Eliot Norton*, 1, p. 342.
3 D. G. Rossetti, letter of 6 March 1856 to William Allingham, *Letters of Dante Gabriel Rossetti*, 1, p. 293.
4 'Something's missing: a discussion between Ernst Bloch and Theodor Adorno on the contributions of Utopian longing' (1964) in Bloch, p. 12; Jameson, p. 63. See also Zipes, 1979; and Hudson, ch. 2, pp. 21–67.
5 On later Pre-Raphaelitism, see J. D. Hunt, Ch. 4, 'Symbolism: the dialectic of a far country', pp. 119–76; Bell, Ch. 3, 'The second generation', pp. 102–77; and Wood, Part 3, 'The later years'.
6 'The sleeping beauty in the wood', *Cornhill magazine*, 13, 1866, p. 559.
7 Heuscher, p. 162. See also Bunce, p. 161; Bloch, pp. 163–6.
8 Brackert and Sander, xxvii. See also Zipes, 1987, p. 5 and Zipes, 1983, pp. 13–44.
9 *Memorials* . . ., 1, p. 84; Lago, p. 179; and 'The late Sir Edward Burne-Jones', *The Spectator*, 3,

652, 25 June 1898, p. 908.
10 Morris, W., 'The lesser arts' in Morris, 1911, 22, p. 6. See also Morris, 'Art and labour', in Morris, 1969, p. 111.
11 Lago, p. 29; Jacobs, p. 131; and Memorials . . ., 2, p. 200.

8

Pre-Raphaelitism,
personification, portraiture
Lewis Johnson

In the chapter of his *Autobiographies* entitled 'Four years: 1887–1891', W. B.
Yeats claims that at this time he was still, as he had been since the
beginning of the 1880s, 'in all things a Pre-Raphaelite' (p. 114). The
possible comprehensiveness of such an affiliation was, however, being
eroded. In 1887 his family had moved back to Bedford Park, the village-
like estate designed in the 1870s by the architect Norman Shaw as if to
replicate and preserve a certain idea of the conditions of English rural life
within the boundaries of the English capital. By the late 1880s, Yeats's
childhood fantasy, established during his family's earlier residence there,
that there was a time 'long ago when the poor were picturesque' (p. 43),
no longer squared with the evidence: the houses on the estate were by
then, it seems, suffering too much decay, too much to defend against the
recognition that the past could not be repeated. Yeats's disappointment
concentrates on the sign hanging outside the estate pub, the Tabard Inn:
the trumpeter painted by Thomas Rooke, assistant to Edward Burne-
Jones, member of the recently formed Society for the Preservation of
Ancient Buildings, had been re-painted. The pub, named after the inn
where Chaucer had staged the assembly of his Canterbury pilgrims, now
seems to admit that the sense of community which Yeats identified with
it was a connotation, nothing concrete, its denoting trumpeter having
required repair.

But Yeats is tenacious. Despite – Yeats almost suggests because of – his
father's rejection of a Pre-Raphaelite painting practice in favour of a more
simple, unadorned portraiture, W. B. maintains his allegiance. ('We must
paint what is in front of us', said John Butler Yeats, rejecting at once both
the historical and symbolic tendencies that had come to be associated
with Pre-Raphaelitism (p. 44).) The disappointment at the failure to
sustain the translation into architectural actuality of a represented medieval past – a practice which Yeats had identified as Pre-Raphaelite[1] – drives

him to hypostatise his fantasies. 'I had made a new religion,' he claims, 'almost an infallible Church of poetic tradition, of a fardel of stories, and of personages, and of emotions . . . .' Infallible because the only law was the support of the certitude of his fantasies. Trying to guarantee that law, Yeats mimes self-quotation:

I had even created a dogma: 'Because those imaginary people are created out of the deepest instinct of man, to be his measure and his norm, whatever I can imagine those mouths speaking may be the nearest I can go to truth.' When I listened they seemed always to speak of one thing only: they, their loves, every incident of their lives, were steeped in the supernatural. (pp. 115–16)

Yeats's tendentious determination of 'the deepest instinct of man' will, we shall see, prove significant. But what is most germane here is his hesitation about what it is that testifies to 'the supernatural'. Who or what speaks to Yeats here? 'They, their loves, every incident of their lives': the pantheon of imaginary beings has to be imagined in action, 'their loves, every incident of their lives', in order that these images can convey to their spectator their lessons, situate Yeats as recipient and transmitter in the 'Church of poetic tradition'.

Which is almost infallible. But not quite. For what supports the translation of image into message, represented figure into speech? Is this what interpretation should accomplish, turning its images into 'a fardel of stories' (a fardel is both a bundle, a little pack, and, figuratively, a burden of sin or sorrow)? Yeats stages his difficulty like this: 'Could even Titian's *Ariosto* that I loved beyond other portraits have its grave look, as if waiting for some perfect final event, if the painters before Titian had not learned portraiture while painting into the corners of compositions full of saints and Madonnas their kneeling patrons?' (p. 116).

Such a portrait seems to resist the translation into narrative, the image accomplishing what was, for Yeats, a paradoxical permanence of the non-supernatural, a simple sustaining of the identifiability of an individual person. The imagined telos of this, when set alongside Yeats's subjectivised version of the 'supernatural', is the promise of that perfect final event: apocalypse, revelation, identity, all co-present. That is – returning to Yeats – the illusion of the identity of image and individual is sustained by his misconstruction of the necessity of the succession, in the shoes of those 'patrons', of singular individuals: those, that is, prepared to display themselves as subject to the representatives of Christian doctrine, the saints and madonnas, providing the tradition in which, and only in which, any identity might be maintained.

If we are to evade this illusion, we must attend to such images differently, noting how the 'individual', or the 'person', is given in action – in Yeats's case, precisely, 'waiting' for that 'final event'. The contention of this chapter is that Yeats's sense of the possibility of turning image into narrative, visual representation into rhetoric, can be extended to reveal that the putative 'genre' of portraiture is, in fact, disparate; that it is never simply a question of who is represented, but what they are represented as; and that this can be revealed interestingly by a reflection on the relationship between portraiture and personification, the latter an example of a rhetorical figure in which any simple idea of the 'person' is subsumed in – what might be called, for now – giving life to a concept.

Further on in the chapter 'Four years: 1887–1891', Yeats relates his encounters with the judgement of the poet W. E. Henley, whom he met and came to know during these years. Yeats used to say of Henley that, as a poet, he was 'like a great actor with a bad part':

I meant that he was like a great actor of passion – character-acting meant nothing to me for many years – and an actor of passion will display some one quality of soul, personified again and again, just as a great poetical painter, Titian, Botticelli, Rossetti, may depend for his greatness upon a type of beauty which presently we call by his name. (p. 125)

The peculiarities of this comparison demonstrate that Yeats's previous account of portraiture, his implied seduction by the possible permanence of identity, was not one which could be sustained, except by illusion. The phrase 'personified again and again', used to describe the activities of a great actor, admits an impermanence of identity even while it obscures it: for the personification of 'some one quality of soul' would, were it not for the suggestion that this one quality might be construed as the very ground and root of the actor's identity, indicate the multiplicity of qualities that identity can be questioned for. And when we seek to understand the implication of Yeats's comparison with the practice of those 'poetical painters', we can see that the cost of his praise of studied repetition is the absorption of the significance of images into the simple carriers of the defining signs of their painter's identities. Like the failed defence against boredom, wandering around a collection in an art gallery: 'This is a Titian . . . this a Botticelli . . . a Rossetti . . . .'

And the failure of such a criticism which calls 'a type of beauty' by the name of a painter becomes all but evident to Yeats further on in his *Autobiographies*. In the chapter entitled 'The tragic generation' he relates how he and his fellow-poets of the Rhymers' Club, meeting in London during the 1890s, tried to maintain a common object of attention and interest, tried to generalise and abstract the significance of their passions, their poetry:

Woman herself was still in our eyes . . ., romantic and mysterious, still the priestess of her shrine, our emotions remembering the Lilith and Sibylla Palmifera of Rossetti; for as yet that sense of comedy which was soon to mould the very fashion-plates, and, in the eyes of men of my generation, to destroy at last the sense of beauty itself, had scarce begun to show here and there, in slight subord-inate touches, among the designs of great painters and craftsmen. (p. 302)

This is, then, the last element in Yeats's self-confessed Pre-Raphaelitism, the final object by which his identity, and those of his colleagues, can be sustained: again a hypostatising, this time of the gender of the figures in Lilith and Sibylla palmifera (1864–68, Delaware Art Museum; 1866–70, Lady Lever Art Gallery, Port Sunlight), their various qualities conjoined in a generic identity of 'woman'. The illusion is, therefore, that 'woman' is already given, that the difference between the sexes is already measured. Yeats is left with simple and inexplicable variation, a diversity guaranteed here by his circle's shared 'sense of beauty'. But the mere possibility of the dispersal of those aspects of 'beauty' in popular fashion threatens the security of their judgement, of their identity. Then, perhaps, 'woman' would reassume a multiple incarnation, many women carrying away the trophies of the ransacked shrine. And, not only is it the case that the dignity of the ideal becomes, under the pressure of the popularising tendencies of art nouveau, for example, impossible to repeat: those previous works come to appear marred by their 'subordinate touches', the turn of a pose, the line of a dress, an amulet, a sceptre loom into prominence, and the imagined common object of Yeats's circle dis-appears.

The rise and fall of Yeats's 'Pre-Raphaelitism' should not be read, then, simply as the lone dispute of an autonomous imagination, inventive as this early and the later Yeats was proved to be. The moments of, and the reasons for, the decline of an identifiable 'Pre-Raphaelitism' were shared with Yeats not only by his circle of poets but also by artists practising in the light of such an allegiance: Burne-Jones, Frederick Sandys, and Ross-etti himself can all be said to have been guided into this as a final defence of their affiliation to a movement. And it is a history which tends to reappear, almost repeating itself, the skeleton of Yeats's near realisations structuring these remarks by L. S. Lowry, who was – perhaps surprisingly – one of this century's most enthusiastic and avid collectors of paintings by Rossetti: 'They're very queer creatures and I like him for it . . . What he puts into the individual is all him, not the individual, they're probably very ordinary people' (A Pre-Raphaelite passion . . ., p. 3). The attenuated sense of mysteriousness of Rossetti's pictures of women (a referent of the first 'they') causes Lowry to wonder not at them nor, with any fascination, at the sitters, but rather at the painter. Once again the variations between Rossetti's pictures of women are assimilated to an idea of his range, his capacity: once again, a Rossetti, several Rossettis. And, what Lowry gives us in return – with the generic 'woman' in which Yeats indulged now under the increasingly embarrassed censure of liberal discourse – is anodyne individuality.

The significance of these moments in the history of criticism of Rossetti's paintings should be drawn out in order to suggest the importance of proceeding to analyse them differently. Lowry's apology for his fascination, for his being enticed into identification with Rossetti as an evasion of the elements of his mystified fascination with those pictures of women, is to reward those pictures with speculation about their sitters. It is not very flattering speculation, granted. But it shares a resemblance with a vein of Pre-Raphaelite criticism, practised at large even recently, which has, either gladly or reluctantly, found itself compensating for that inconvenient embarrassment at what appears to be the egomaniacal repetitiousness of Rossetti's paintings of women by setting out to do a different justice to his sitters. That justice takes the form of two moves which Lowry's remark exemplifies: all that is evident in Rossetti's pictures is the power or domination (these values differ, of course) of his fantasy: consequently, reluctantly or militantly (power apologising for itself, or domination being fought), the painter's supposed non-recognition of the 'individuality' of his sitters is repaired. Whether this takes the form of Lowry's unflattering speculation, or the often inconsequential bon mot which characterises much of the research published in the recent joint publication by the Tate Gallery and Penguin Books, The Pre-Raphaelites (1984), or the more dedicated and systematic collation of the circumstances, characteristics and activities of the women who, in part, were the models for the paintings, as is evinced in Jan Marsh's The Pre-Raphaelite sisterhood (1985), the tendency is there. Solipsism and atomic individuality; little question of, let alone model of, intersubjectivity.

The virtue, then, of a symptomatic reading of Yeats's 'Pre-Raphaelitism', its place in the development, indeed, of his notorious solipsism and his ideal of autonomous individuality,[2] is to try to place the rhetoric of the last element of that affiliation, that last common object of his and his circle's fantasy, that awkward 'woman': 'Woman herself was still in our eyes . . ., romantic and mysterious, still the priestess of her shrine, our emotions remembering the Lilith and Sibylla Palmifera of Rossetti.' But let us note that the subject of his sentence is not simply 'woman' but 'woman herself'. And this is not merely emphatic. It crosses the whole problem, the general and the particular. Yeats's 'woman herself' appears as the consequence of the interrupted interpretation of such pictures as *Lilith* and *Sibylla palmifera*: 'Who do these women appear as?' is cast aside in favour of the specious generality 'woman', particularised – so as not to require any more elaborate identification, her shrine an altar in no systematic church or faith – by the 'herself'. That this is not simply the consequence of a simple sum of the sins of omitting to recognise 'individuals' should, therefore, be clear. What is less clear is how to continue that interpretation, asking the question who do these women appear as, so that the illusion of 'woman herself' remaining in their eyes – the imaginary stuck with this symbol – can be dissolved.

In the rest of this chapter, I shall outline one way in which attentiveness to the rhetoric of the description and interpretation of visual images, those forms of language used to identify and elaborate visual representations, can provide us not simply with a symptomatology of the misreadings of others – as in the account of Yeats and Lowry above – but, further, with an understanding of the necessary limits of the communicability of visual experience. Paradoxically, however, this turns out to entail an argument, precisely, for the necessity of communicating, the obligation to offer, some account of that experience.

A part of the definition of 'personification' in the *Shorter Oxford English Dictionary* reads: 'An imaginary person conceived as representing a thing or abstraction.' It gives 1850 as the date of the first usage of this implied definition.[3] It is a cogent description of the rhetorical figure employed by Yeats in his interpretation of Rossetti's *Lilith* and *Sibylla palmifera*. It is also, interestingly enough, a cogent description of the rhetorical figure employed by John Ruskin in a famous passage that concludes volume one of his *Modern painters* (1843) and which he had repeated in the preface to *Pre-Raphaelitism* (1851), his extended defence of the rising lights of contemporary English painting. 'The young artists of England', he writes, '. . . should go to nature in all singleness of heart, and walk with her laboriously and trustingly, having no other thought but how best to penetrate her meaning, rejecting nothing, selecting nothing, and scorning nothing' (*Pre-Raphaelitism*, 12, p. 339). Ruskin's figure seems to be a response to an aspect of 'Pre-Raphaelitism' (the coherence of the movement as movement being what is here, exactly, in question) which is at the furthest possible remove from Yeats's. Nonetheless, it employs an identical figure; personification being admitted to solve the difficulty of communicating two radically different limits of the effect of Pre-Raphaelite images on nineteenth-century eyes.

So, while Yeats appears to be hanging on to some means of evading the source of his seduction by Rossetti's style, holding out against the collapse of his engagement with those different paintings of women into either a multiple pantheon of goddesses or constituency of many women, Ruskin appears to be responding to the more objective grounds of the construction of the initial 'movement'. At one extreme, the absorption of the significance of 'Pre-Raphaelitism' into fantasy; at another, the defence against the recognition that the programme of the accumulation of discrete data of visual experience – which Ruskin had elaborated with more and more commitment as Modern painters grew from one volume into five[4] – had no guarantee of objectivity. At both extremes, the '-ism' of 'Pre-Raphaelitism', the second very much the shared guarantee of the brotherhood itself.[5]

But if such a conception of the epistemological pretensions of a practice of visual representation as Ruskin advances in Modern painters cannot be supported, not least because it produces such a personification of nature, then that is all the more reason to examine in some detail what we might call some lower-order personifications, ones which respond not to this questioning of the condition of the saturation of the eye that this – and other – varieties of 'realism' tend to promote, but to other conditions of the relations between seeing and saying.

It has been argued that Ford Madox Brown's Work (1852, 1856–63; Manchester City Art Galleries) should be considered as an extended, a multiple personification of the concept of work (Open University, pp. 80–7). It has also, though, been analysed – in Linda Nochlin's book Realism (1973, pp. 127–30) – as the then most systematic fulfilment, in England, of a practice of realism in painting. She takes full account of the choice of subject, the style, its apparent purpose in its meticulousness of making present, in quasi-simultaneity, a full range of actors in a cross-section of English society. How, though, does this square with the argument that the painting should, so the personification argument goes, be viewed as providing a theatre of figures engaged in, or disengaged from, the practice of labour? That is, the representation is viewed as a making visible of a concept, a making visible – it should be stressed – which demonstrates the necessary fragmentation, in mid-nineteenth-century England, of this concept of work, this form of energia: the workmen, the woman looking after the children, the intellectuals (conventionally identified as F. D. Maurice and Thomas Carlyle) and, of course, the rich hangers-on and the disenfranchised poor.

Care should, then, be taken. As Brown wrote in the catalogue to his 1865 one-man show, an occasion largely dedicated to the display of this painting, 'the British excavator' in the foreground (perhaps the one standing or the one crouching – it is not quite clear) should be considered as 'the outward and visible type of *Work*' (*The Pre-Raphaelites*, no. 88; his italics). And we can interpret Brown as alerting us to the other, less obviously visible types of work. (I have, for example, included the woman looking after the children in the previous list of 'workers', stretching an interesting point out of Brown's account in so doing.) But, it should be asked, is it not prejudicial to determine this or that labourer-figure as expressing completely, or simply instantiating the concept of 'work', as Brown's phrase 'the outward and visible type' suggests we do? If work should be admitted as an abstract idea to which such a figure stands in some relation, then it must always be a question of relation, not of incarnation. And the reading off of the meaning of these labourer-figures, either from Brown's account or in order to assemble an ideal cast of some 'cross-section' of the then contemporary English society, simply repeats his occlusion of other forms of engagement with them. Is this not what justice requires for and of the recognition of the disadvantages that labour labours under?

We might ask similar questions of another famous Pre-Raphaelite work, Holman Hunt's *The light of the world* (**4**) (1851–53, 1856, 1886; Keble College, Oxford). We would be dealing, of course, with a far less generally recognised concept than in the case of *Work*, but there are good grounds for considering 'The light of the world' as necessarily an abstraction. Characteristic interpretations of this haloed figure carrying a lantern and standing, knocking at the door into (or out of?) a garden, have tended – as befits this, perhaps the most popular Protestant icon – to identify him as, indeed, 'The light of the world', its personification. This nomination of the figure, this slide between title and image, tends however to disguise the means to signification of the visual form of Hunt's argument. When he wrote in what was called – exactly – his 'Apology for the symbolism introduced into the picture called 'The Light of the World' of 1865: 'He who when in body was the LIGHT OF THE WORLD could not be unprovided when in the Spirit, with the means of guiding his followers when it was night' (*The Pre-Raphaelites*, no. 57), he demonstrates that the significance of the setting is to reverse the metaphoric value of night. In the picture, now it is night, Christ – presumably the resurrected Christ – regains that condition of being the illuminator of the world that Hunt claims, in his commentary, that he was when he was alive, in body. And the much argued-over significance of the form of the lamp that he is carrying – usually identified as a multiple synecdoche, a collocation of various different window forms, signalling a synthesis of their corresponding churches – is revealed, as is Hunt's meticulousness about the construction of the model for it, as the delay of this recognition of the tendentious relation between figure and setting. Thus does Hunt's work invite an attention which is lost between the identification of detailed elements and a minor rapture in the sight of Christ, a discreet displacement of the ban on Protestant icons.

But both Brown's *Work* and Hunt's *The light of the world* are only perso-nifications *à rebours*. In order, then, to situate what I wish to uncover about the relation between this rhetorical figure and Rossetti's works, a brief consideration of the practice and theory of his near contemporary, George Frederic Watts, will allow us better to comprehend Rossetti's deviation from more direct forms of visual personification. For Watts was the most dedicated of mid- to late nineteenth-century practitioners of painted personification.

A brief list of titles: as well as *Love and death*, illustrated here (**25**), we have, as its companion, *Love and life*; we have similar figure compositions *Time and oblivion*, *Time unveiling truth* and *Time, death and judgement*; we have the large fresco, *Justice: a hemicycle of lawgivers*, with over thirty figures presided over by those of Truth, Justice and Mercy, in the Hall at Lincoln's Inn college of law; we have *Hope, Chaos, Destiny*.[6] And it is interesting to reflect that, contrary to the simple received opinion about Watts's works, these personifications of abstract concepts are not, by and large, matched by a repetition of a more properly classical pantheon. There are the sculptures of the classical goddesses or characters Clytie, Daphne and Medusa[7] – a medium and a form of representation which in Watts's hands tends to minimise the opportunity for the simple transmission of the received identities of these figures and which, instead, draws us first into an engagement with movement and action, rather than symbol or sche-matic attribute – but there is no systematic reiteration of a classical cast.

This relative absence of painted or sculpted representations of classical figures, and instead the multiplication of more common general con-cepts, should be viewed in the light of the widespread revivification of those classical personages in the public art, particularly sculpture, of the Victorian era.[8] Watts's practice is to segregate concept and image, avoid their too easy interchange in the vocabulary of classical learning, work to try to redetermine the qualifications for participation in a public for art.

Indeed a pictorial vocabulary which so partakes of traditional academic forms invites a simple identification, by name, of the figures, too easily thought of as the proper subjects of art. But, instead, we are drawn towards the improbabilities of thinking of oblivion as a figure, love as a little boy, death as an elegantly draped woman. What if one habitually thought of figures who could not be identified by name, whose signs of identifiability were so reduced, in shadow, in colour, in obscurity, as the limit concepts of our thought? A recipe for paranoia. Watts's *representations* are a labour against this state, turning the anxieties about the qualifications for participation in that public art into the first ground of belonging to a public.

Watts left a small archive of writings, most of them accounts and defences of his pictorial practice, which were collated, edited and published by his second wife, Mary, as *Thoughts on art*, the third volume of three of mixed biography and documentary material. Watts argues at one point that 'The wide range of modern thought requires a wide range of suggestions, significance, and appeal' and, elsewhere, he defends the means he has used to respond to this circumstance, to produce forms which will mediate these fragments:

I have used human forms because there are no other by which it would be at all possible to suggest ideas belonging to human conditions, but I have purposely abstained from any attempt to make the figures seem real, or vividly to awaken recollections of reality, feeling the necessity of the atmosphere of remoteness, and knowing that familiarity produces a sense of the commonplace. (Watts, 3, p. 36)

Note here, for example, the plural 'human conditions': not a claim for the supra-historical significance of his work, dealing even as it does with such things as are easily imagined to be permanent fundamentals; but a recognition of the different conditions of viewing, different relations between viewers and those general concepts. Thus, perhaps, one might say that in *Love and death* the boy reaches out to caress the woman; another, that he reaches out to defend himself from her. Is his expression one of awe or fear? Love solicits, heralds, or seeks to defeat death? That, then, which can be gathered under the name of love or death aggregates; fragments move into series.

Love and death (**25**), painted in the late 1870s and early 1880s, is one of Watts's more successful allegories. The problem with its companion piece, *Love and life*, and with the well-known painting *Hope* might be summarised as follows: the suggestion of inaction, the obscurity of what might be, has been or will be taking place, does not allow one to understand those concepts as subject to change, to realisation or to dispute. A naked girl on a rocky peak with a man above her holding her hands, him naked too save for a great pair of wings – is this life helping love up, the other way round, or is there only hindrance? And why is Hope found sat on top of such a solitary peak? Perhaps we would say that hope is often isolated, a lonely and improbable defiance. But why or how this might be the case we are none the wiser. (A symptomatic reading would reveal that the identifiability of the figures was too untroubled, involving little checking, little in the way of revision: vision producing, apparently without labour, figures and objects ready for their names. Name them as girl, as man – why rename them love or life? The movements of identification occluded, visual representation appears as if always already a code, its place as imaginary resolution of dispute rendered almost imperceptible.)

Watts's practice of representing figures personifying concepts in action can be set against his practice as a portraitist. The failure of certain of his allegories bears a crucial relation to the following determination of the form of the portrait: 'A portrait should have in it something of the monumental; it is a summary of the life of the person, not the record of accidental position, or arrangement of light and shadow . . . Also, if a single figure, it should appear capable of action but performing none' (p. 35). These conditions evoke the impossible. Watts's syntax here allows us to erase the simple necessity of such a portrait being an arrangement of light and shadow: the absence of either a definite or indefinite article (i.e. 'the . . .' or 'an arrangement') invites us to imagine that light and shadow are simply epiphenomenal to the representation of the person, that they are, like that 'position', simply 'accidental', that it is not their differentiation which permits the emergence of figure from ground. Inspection of Watts's portraits – the many, for example, collected at the National Portrait Gallery in London – demonstrates that none of this is so. Faces often turned aside, emerging as if with difficulty from the dark background in which their bodies tend to be swallowed; this difficulty amounting to diffidence as their gaze is withheld from us. The careful deliberations that have balanced these faces and figures in a suspension between unidentifiability and what appears to have been an undesirable boldness of sitter–viewer address belie the hidden sense of Watts's syntax: not only are light and shadow required by the simple fact of representation, but their modulation is inseparable from the precise articulation of the claim of these figures on our attention. Faces like these, likenesses – so the documentation suggests – of Thomas Carlyle,

25 G. F. Watts, *Love and death*

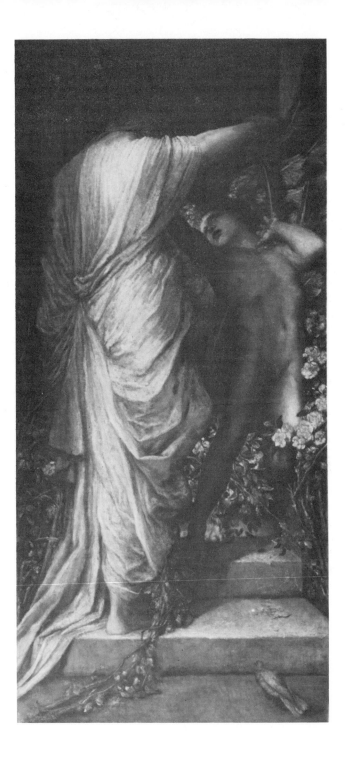

or J. S. Mill, or Cecil Rhodes, eyes set on the floor or gazing off into space, tend not to confront us. It is a subtle strategy: that absence of direct address, and the carefully minimal articulation of the elements that compose a likeness combine to invite the search for a *name*.

But such a search might go too fast. Like Watts's legislating that 'if a single figure, it should appear capable of action but performing none', we might miss that action of the emergence of the face and of the body, that very emergence which is inseparable from the emergence of the conditions of identifiability of that figure. Perhaps our eye misses the response of the gaze of the sitter; perhaps it is too used to the portrait form, saturated, all too ready to grant that this is someone. And so, as the almost consuming shadows of Watts's portraits threaten to absorb our capacity to tolerate indifference, we escape to the name. And if we forget these manoeuvres, we can hardly fail to be surprised that the modesty of the pose belongs to a figure of such reputation. And we might forget the very role that such a portrait has taken in forming and reforming that name.

The separation, then, in Watts's work between portraits and personifications receives false justification. Indeed, the separation between them cannot be absolute: that which allows for the effectiveness of his allegories as an antidote to paranoia and that which admits the possibility that his portraits might promote it (that awful parade of heroes) is, simply, the practice of visual representation.

This division between portraits and personifications and allegories in Watts's career was pursued by him, far from reluctantly, to the extent that it was his donation in 1886 of a large quantity of his portraits to the National Portrait Gallery that precipitated its move from an enclave in the Bethnal Green Museum to the specially constructed building in St Martin's Place, just off Trafalgar Square, in 1895. His pursuit of likenesses of important contemporaries had been part of the very movement which had resulted in the legal constitution of the gallery in 1856, nearly forty years before.

Thus, in contrast, Rossetti's personifications-cum-portraits. Hence their relation to the dispute pursued as part of the constitution and maintenance of the identity of the Pre-Raphaelites, their rejection of the genres around which official painting was being organised and presented – the divergence of Rossetti's so-called style, in these works of the late 1850s onwards, being rather beside the point. But that is not to affirm that he or the rest of the Pre-Raphaelites thought so. By then, the Brotherhood had been dissolved, its members all too ready to differ about the question of styles which they might try to make their own. And yet, as the above account of Yeats's fascinated Pre-Raphaelitism demonstrates, there was a content to that trend, unrecognised though it tended to be. With what that '-ism' obscured we shall here conclude.

A work by Rossetti of 1871–72 known as *The bower meadow* (**27**) was, in the course of being painted, altered. Instead of representing, in the foreground, two women – as he put it – 'playing music, while Love holds a song bird whose music chimes with theirs', it shows, beyond those two foreground figures, two women dancing together and, in the further distance, another coming this way, carrying a basket over her shoulder. The figure of love has disappeared and, as the title claims, we are referred not to any relation between these female figures and that concept, but simply (and rather unusually for Rossetti) to the setting. The multiple reference of 'bower' – either an abode, or more archaically a boudoir, or even a player of a stringed instrument – indicates that Rossetti's multiplication of women and the omission of the figure of love signifies, even as it might promise a domain of female rule, a limitation of that domain to a meadow-abode or meadow-boudoir. Rossetti evades the representation of those female figures together with that figure of love, and suggests instead a confinement of women to nature and, yet, to the bedroom.

A possible exception to this evasion of the depiction of female figures in some relation to a figure of love is *Beata Beatrix* (*c*. 1864–70; Tate Gallery). In his account of this picture, Rossetti claims that he has painted, beyond the figure of the woman seated in the foreground, the figures of Dante and of love. This image, variously described since as of a woman in extreme pain or pleasure, should, claims Rossetti: '. . . be viewed not as a representation of the incident of the death of Beatrice, but as an ideal of the subject, symbolized by a trance or sudden spiritual transfiguration' (*The Pre-Raphaelites*, no. 131). Rossetti's commentary continues, indicating that he has conceived that, in the hand of love, towards whom Dante is gazing, 'the waning life of his lady flickers as a flame'. The trouble with this determination of the 'allegorical' significance of *Beata Beatrix* is that Rossetti appears to have determined the degrees of activity of the various figures in exactly the wrong proportions. He suggests that the figure of Beatrice languishes in neither pain nor pleasure but, instead, in a 'symbolized' trance. And yet the figure of love holds the key – despite the fact that very little seems to be happening back there – to what will happen. Thus he evades determining what is supposed to denote this connoted 'spiritual trance', even while the very identification of the figure at the back as love insinuates some such suggestion as the condition of the

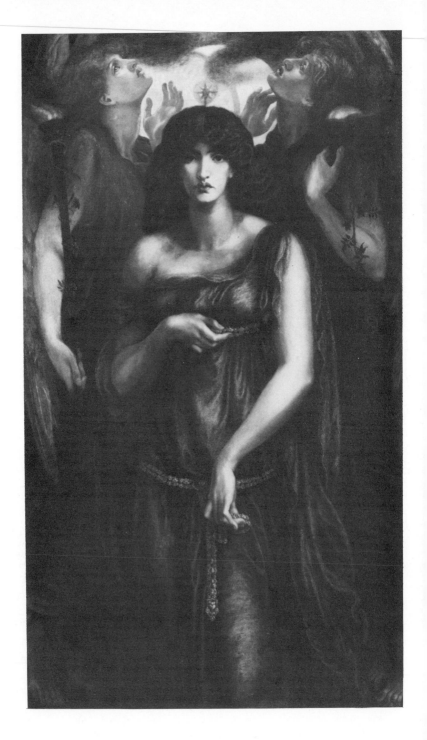

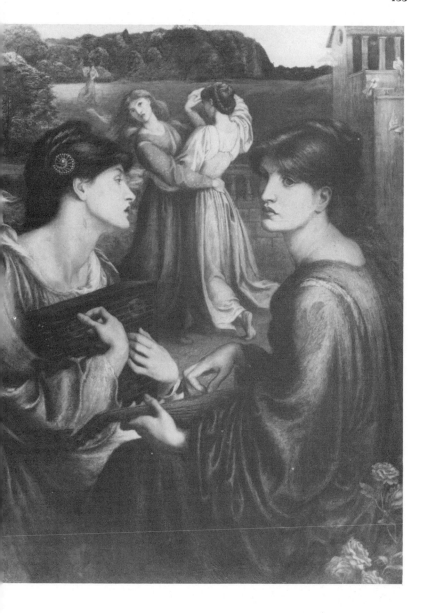

D. G. Rossetti: (facing) **26** *Astarte Syriaca*; (this page) **27** *The bower meadow*

suspension of this woman's fate. Rossetti's painting, then, of the death of his wife allows him to encourage us that it was not really a fate that she – whoever she might have been – was subject to.

The failure to recognise who she might have been, that she was subject to death, seems to have allowed Rossetti to hold in suspension the possibility of the self-identity of the women he painted and to indulge multiple identifications of such painted figures. Hence such identifications of female figures as Watts tended to avoid (Cupid would, for example, be the affiliated model of love in Love and death), Rossetti tended to cultivate.

If, though, we look closely at Astarte Syriaca (**26**) in the light of another of his verbal interpretations, this time the sonnet he wrote for the picture, the last six lines of which he had incorporated into the frame of the picture, we can see that such an identification is highly unstable. The sonnet reads:

> Mystery: lo! betwixt the Sun and Moon
> Astarte of the Syrians: Venus Queen
> Ere Aphrodite was. In silver sheen
> Her twofold girdle clasps the infinite boon
> Of bliss whereof Heaven and Earth commune:
> And from her neck's inclining flower-stem lean
> Love-freighted lips and absolute eyes that wean
> The pulse of hearts to the sphere's dominant tune.
>
> Torch-bearing, her sweet ministers compel
> All thrones of light beyond the sky and sea
> The witnesses of Beauty's face to be:
> That face, of love's all-penetrative spell
> Amulet, talisman, and oracle, –
> Betwixt the Sun and Moon a mystery. (The Pre-Raphaelites, no. 147)

This version of the picture tends, as the use of the sestet in the frame's cartouche suggests, to divide. And across that division, a near repetition of interpretative moves demonstrates something of the function of the picture's form in permitting not an identification of an individual, not a portrait, but the supension of a judgement – like that by Yeats, by Lowry – of visual pleasure.

The tendency towards repetition – this is Astarte, these her ministers, she is, they are – which Rossetti's use of only half the sonnet appears to encourage is, though, secondary to the production of a confusion of identities. The opening lines, with their archaic 'betwixt', suggest that we can identify the figures to the left and right as the Sun and Moon. The 'lo!' encourages us to do so. But, by the end of the sonnet, we are being encouraged to differentiate between those figures, Astarte's torch-bearing 'sweet-ministers', and the Sun and the Moon, these latter now seeming to be those 'thrones of light' which are compelled by those figures to be witnesses of 'Beauty's face'. Hence the emphatic 'That face . . .' at the beginning of the antipenultimate line: without it, we would be far less inclined to decide that the face facing ours was, indeed, that of 'Beauty'. As it is, this hesitation about the identity of the figures either side of Astarte, the instability of the consequent reidentification of the main figure as Beauty, the possibility of construing her as that *and* as love, she the very source of her own power (as 'the infinite boon / Of bliss' we are promised earlier), demonstrates the importance of the visual form both as a sort of classical archaeology and a search for defining characteristics associated with a portrait.

The archaism, then, of the symmetry of the composition – Rossetti getting very Pre-Raphaelite – which is vital in encouraging the search for classical and, in this case, pre-classical nominations, also tends to reduce the possibility of interpreting the figures as animated. And that apparent near absence of movement and identifiable action invites – as we saw in the case of Watts's idea of an actionless portrait – the characteristic response that, well, this is an investigation of the likeness of Jane Morris. Thus Rossetti seems to have it both ways: an investigation of concepts and of likeness.

In a letter dated 23 August 1869 Rossetti wrote to Jane Morris about the possibility of her sitting for him when she returned from the German spa of Ems where she was 'taking the cure': 'I have been conceiving a great desire to paint you as Fortune and have the design clearly in my head now, having long been knocking it about there' (*Rossetti–Morris correspondence*, p. 25). Strange locution, 'I have been conceiving a great desire': him the agent, the mother, of his own desires? Thus such a design functions: illusion of intention and of the authority of the artist to prejudge the limits of imagination. Hence, again, idea and likeness, separate and together.

Astarte Syriaca (1875–77) (**26**) is, I think, the best example of these hesitations, this having things both ways before they are there to be had. But there are many other examples of paintings of women by Rossetti which – if his interpretations of them are followed or repeated, as they were by Yeats and by Lowry – contain them, miss their significance. For what they demonstrate is the absence of any extended series of conditions under which these women of the mid- and late nineteenth century might have been recognised. What, though, is further demonstrated – by this consideration of the relations between portraiture and personification – is that, even while such interpretations seek to contain such images, those paintings function to expose the limitations of the field of action available to those women, and the limitations of any more narrowly defined concept of political representation.

Notes

1 The relations between the Pre-Raphaelites and medieval revivalism have often been contentious ones: a too-close association would dissolve some aspects of the distinctiveness of their 1848 break, set their medievalism in continuity with the already well-under-way Gothic revival; a complete severance though, such as is encouraged by the neglect of this issue in recent criticism, is obviously unwarrantable. What is required is a consideration of the *functions* of their represented past: so, while Rossetti's paintings of Arthurian subjects such as *Arthur's tomb* (1855; British Museum) tend to de-realise that past, place it as an irrecoverable intensity of 'feeling', the watercolours of G. P. Boyce (see Tate Gallery, *G. P. Boyce*, London, 1987), with their preoccupation with the architectural remains of feudalism, tend to promise a reintegration of that past, an assimilation with a present, benign and protective. The relations – in the plural – are therefore exactly contentious.

2 Cf. Leavis, pp. 27–50, esp. pp. 40–1 for an (unexplained) account of this.

3 With this 'An imaginary person conceived as representing a thing or abstraction' of 1850, cf. Marx, Bk. 1, Part 1, Ch. 1, Sec. 4.

4 See my forthcoming *Prospects, thresholds, interiors: British watercolours from the Victoria and Albert Museum*, Miami, 1989.

5 E.g. the subtitle to their magazine *The Germ*, i.e. *Thoughts towards nature in literature and art* – 'towards' being the operative and convenient word.

6 Respectively: 1887, Tate Gallery; 1893, Musée de Louvre; 1848, Eastnor Castle; c. 1851–52, Little Holland House (now destroyed, but illustrated in Barrington, f.p. 112); c. 1865, Sheffield City Art Galleries; 1853–59, Hall of Lincoln's Inn, London; 1886, Tate Gallery; 1875–82, Watts Gallery, Compton (on loan from Fitzwilliam Museum, Cambridge); 1904, Watts Gallery.

7 Respectively: c. 1868, Watts Gallery; 1879–82, Tate Gallery; c. 1844, Watts Gallery.

8 See Marina Warner, esp. pp. 45–60, for a good account of this tendency and a critical diagnosis of its connections with contemporary revivals of 'Victorianism' in both contemporary conservatism and the contemporary art market.

Bibliography

Allingham, W., *A Diary*, ed. H. Allingham, and D. Radford, New York, 1985

Bann, S., 'How revolutionary is the new art history?' in A. L. Rees and F. Borzello eds, *The new art history*, London, 1986, pp. 19–31

Barker, D. L., 'The regulation of marriage: repressive benevolence' in G. Littlejohn, B. Smart, J. Wakeford and N. Yuval-Davis, eds., *Power and the state*, London, 1978

Barrington, Mrs R., ed., *G. F. Watts: reminiscences*, London, 1905

Barthes, R., 'The death of the author' in *Image, music, text*, trans. S. Heath, London, 1977, pp. 142–8

Bartram, M., *The Pre-Raphaelite camera, aspects of Victorian photography*, London, 1985

Baudrillard, J., *For a critique of the political economy of the sign*, trans. C. Levin, St Louis, Mo., 1981

de Beauvoir, S., *The second sex* (1949), Harmondsworth, 1983

Bell, Q., *A new and noble school: the Pre-Raphaelites*, London, 1982

Benjamin, W., *Charles Baudelaire: a lyric poet in the era of high capitalism*, trans. H. Zohn, London, 1973

Bennett, M., *Ford Madox Brown 1821–1893*, Manchester City Art Gallery, 1965

Bennett, M., *William Holman Hunt*, Walker Art Gallery, Liverpool and Victoria and Albert Museum, London, 1969

Best, G., *Mid-Victorian Britain, 1851–1875* (1971), London, 1985

Bhaba, H., 'Sly civility', October, 34, fall 1985

Bloch, E., *The utopian function of art and literature*, trans. J. Zipes and F. Mecklenburg, Cambridge, Mass. and London, 1988

G. P. Boyce, Tate Gallery, London, 1987

Brackert, H. and Sander, V., eds., *German fairy tales*, New York, 1984

Brewster, D., *A treatise on new philosophical instruments for various purposes in the arts and sciences. With experiments on light and colours*, London, 1813

Brewster, D., *A treatise on the kaleidoscope*, Edinburgh, 1819

Brewster, D., *The stereoscope, its history, theory, and construction*, London, 1856

Brewster, D., *Letters on natural magic addressed to Sir Walter Scott*, London, 1834, new edn. with introductory chapters by J. A. Smith, London, 1856

Bronkhurst, J., *William Holman Hunt, Catalogue raisonné*, Yale University Press, forthcoming

Buckley, J. H., *The Victorian temper: a study in literary culture*, New York, 1951

Bulwer-Lytton, R., Baroness, *Behind the scenes*, London, 1854

Bunce, J. T., *Fairy tales: their origin and meaning*, New York and London, 1987

Burgan, M., 'Heroines at the piano: women and music in nineteenth-century fiction', *Victorian studies*, 30, autumn 1986, pp. 51–76

Carlyle, T., 'Biography' (1832), *Critical and miscellaneous essays*, 4 (1839), 1869

Casteras, S., *The substance and the shadow*, New Haven, Conn., 1982

Casteras, S., 'John Everett Millais's "secret-looking garden wall' and the courtship barrier in Victorian painting' in A. Munich ed., *Victorian women and men*, New York, Browning Institute Studies, 1986

Casteras, S., *Images of victorian womanhood in English art*, Rutherford, NJ, 1987

Cecil, D., *Visionary and dreamer, two poetic painters: Samuel Palmer and Edward Burne-Jones*, Princeton, NJ, 1969

Cellini, B., *Autobiography of Benvenuto Cellini*, 1728, trans. J. A. Symonds, New York, 1960

Cerda i Surroca, M. A., *Els Pre-Raphaelites a Catalunyá: una literatura i uns simbols*, Barcelona, 1981

Cherry, D. and Pollock, G., 'Woman as sign in Pre-Raphaelite literature: a study of the representation of Elizabeth Siddal', *Art history*, June 1984, pp. 206–77

Cherry, D. and Pollock, G., 'Patriarchal history and the Pre-Raphaelites', *Art history*, December 1984, pp. 480–95

Chesneau, E., *La peinture anglaise*, Paris, 1882

Claudet, A., 'Photography in its relation to the fine arts', *The photographic journal*, 6, 15 June 1860

Collins, W., *Basil*, 1852, revised 1862, Toronto and London, 1980

Coombs, J. H., Scott, A. M., Landow, G. P. and Sanders, A. A., *A Pre-Raphaelite friendship: the correspondence of William Holman Hunt and John Lucas Tupper*, Ann Arbor, Mich., 1986

Cunningham, A., *The life of David Wilkie*, London, 1843

Darnton, R., 'The meaning of Mother Goose', *New York review of books*, 31: 1, February 1984, p. 44

Davidoff, L. and Hall, C., *Family fortunes: men and women of the English middle class*, 1780–1850, Tiptree, 1987

Delamotte, P., ed., *The sunbeam: a book of photographs from nature*, London, 1859

Delaware Art Museum, *The Samuel and Mary R. Bancroft, Jr., and related Pre-Raphaelite collections of the Delaware art museum* (1978), revised 1984

Dickens, C., *David Copperfield* (1849–50), Oxford, 1981

Dickens, C., *Nicholas Nickleby* (1839), Harmondsworth, 1978

Faberman, H., 'Augustus Egg's self-portrait as a poor author', *The Burlington magazine*, 125, April 1983

Fearn, J., *An appeal to philosophers, by name, on the demonstration of vision in the brain, and against the attack of Sir David Brewster, on the rationale of cerebral vision*, London, 1837

Fellows, J., *The failing distance: the autobiographical impulse in John Ruskin*, Baltimore, Md and London, 1975

Fitzgerald, P., *Edward Burne-Jones: a biography*, London, 1975

Flint, K., 'The woman reader and the opiate of fiction: 1855–1870' in J. Hawthorne, ed., *The nineteenth-century British novel*, London, 1986, pp. 47–61

Fredeman, W. E., *Pre-Raphaelitism: a bibliocritical study*, London, 1965

Freud, S., *The Pelican Freud Library*, Harmondsworth, 1973–

Gernsheim, H. and A., *The history of photography from the camera obscura to the beginning of the modern era*, New York, 1969

Gillis, J. R., *For better, for worse. British marriages, 1600 to the present*, New York and Oxford, 1985

Great Victorian pictures: their paths to fame, London, 1978

Greenhill, G., 'The death of Chatterton, or photography and the law', *History of photography*, 5, 1981, pp. 199–205

Greg, W. R., 'Prostitution', *Westminster review*, 103, 1850, pp. 448–506

Grieve, A., 'The Pre-Raphaelite Brotherhood and the anglican high church', *Burlington magazine*, 111, May 1969, p. 294

Grieve, A., *The art of Dante Gabriel Rossetti* (1. Found; 2. *The Pre-Raphaelite modern life subject*), Norwich, 1976

Grilli, S., 'The Pre-Raphaelites and phrenology' in L. Parris, ed., *Pre-Raphaelite papers*, London, 1984

Harrison, M. and Waters, B., *Burne-Jones*, London, 1973

Helsinger, E., *Ruskin and the art of the beholder*, Cambridge, Mass., 1982

Heuscher, J. E., 'Briar rose: the sleeping beauty' in *A psychiatric study of myths and fairy tales*, Springfield, Ill., 1974

Hewison, R., *The argument of the eye*, London, 1976

Holcomb, L., 'Victorian wives and property: reform of the married women's property law, 1857–1882', in M. Vicinus ed., *A widening sphere: changing roles of Victorian women*, Bloomington, Ind. and London, 1977

Horkheimer, M., and Adorno, T., *Dialectic of enlightenment*, trans. J. Cumming, New York, 1987

Hudson, W., *The marxist philosophy of Ernst Bloch*, London, 1982

Humphreys, H. N., *The origin and progress of the art of writing*, London, 1853

Hunt, Diana Holman, *My Grandfather: his wives and loves*, London, (1969), 1987

Hunt, J. D., 'Symbolism: "the dialectic of a far country" ' in *The Pre-Raphaelite imagination 1848–1900*, London, 1968

Hunt, W. H., 'Notes of the life of Augustus L. Egg', *Reader*, 1, 1863, pp. 462, 486–7, 557–8; 2, 1863, pp. 42–3, 91, 516–17; 3, 1864, pp. 56–7

Hunt, W. H., *The miracle of the Holy Fire in the church of the sepulchre at Jerusalem, painted by W. Holman Hunt*, n.d. (London, 1900)

Hunt, W. H., *Pre-Raphaelitism and the Pre-Raphaelite Brotherhood*, London, 1905

Ironside, R. and Gere, J., *Pre-Raphaelite Painters*, London, 1948

Jacobs, J., 'Some recollections of Sir Edward Burne-Jones', *The nineteenth century*, 45, 1899, p. 131

Jameson, F., *The political unconscious: narrative as a socially symbolic act*, Ithaca, NY, 1981

Johnson, L., *Prospects, thresholds, interiors: British watercolours from the Victoria and Albert Museum*, Miami, 1989

Keats, J., *The poetical works of John Keats*, London, 1956

Khnopff, F., 'A tribute from Belgium', *The magazine of art*, 22, 1898, p. 525

Kingsley, C., *Charles Kingsley, his letters and memories of his life, edited by his wife*, London, 1899

Lacan, J., *Ecrits, a selection*, trans. A. Sheridan, London, 1977

Lacan, J., *The four fundamental concepts of psychoanalysis*, trans., A. Sheridan, London, 1977

Lago, M., ed., *Burne-Jones talking: his conversations 1895–1898 preserved by his studio assistant Thomas Rooke*, London, 1982

Landow, G. P., *The aesthetic and critical theories of John Ruskin*, Princeton, NJ, 1971

Landow, G. P., 'William Holman Hunt's "The shadow of death" ', *Bulletin of the John Rylands Library of Manchester*, autumn 1972, 55,1

Landow, G. P., *Holman and typological symbolism*, New Haven, Conn. and London,

1979

Landow, G. P., 'William Holman Hunt's "Oriental mania" and his Uffizzi "self portrait", *Art bulletin*, December 1982'

Landow, G. P., 'Shadows cast by "The light of the world": William Holman Hunt's religious paintings, 1893–1905', *Art bulletin*, September 1983

Lane, E. W., *An account of the manners and customs of the modern Egyptians*, 2 vols., London, 1836

Laycock, T., *A treatise on the nervous diseases of women*, London, 1840

Leavis, F. R., *New bearings in English poetry*, London, 1950

Leonard, P., *Personality and ideology: towards a materialist understanding of the individual*, London, 1984

Lottes, W., *Wie ein goldener traum*, Munich, 1984

Lüthi, M., *Once upon a time: on the nature of fairy tales*, trans. L. Chadeayne and P. Gottwald, Bloomington, Ind., 1976

Maas, J., *Holman Hunt and 'the light of the world'*, London, 1984

Marsh, J. *The Pre-Raphaelite sisterhood*, London, 1985

Marx, K., *Capital: a critique of political economy*, trans. B. Fowkes, (Harmondsworth, 1976), New York, 1977

Mayo, H., *Outlines of human physiology*, London, 1837

Meisel, M., *Realisations*, Princeton, NJ, 1983

Memorials of Edward Burne-Jones, ed. G. B. J. (Georgiana Burne-Jones), London, 1904

Millais, J. G., *The life and letters of Sir John Everett Millais*, London, 1899

Morawski, S., *Inquiries into the fundamentals of aesthetics*, Cambridge, Mass. and London, 1974

Morris, W. *Collected works*, ed. M. Morris, London, 1911

Morris, W., *The unpublished lectures of William Morris*, ed. E. D. Le Mire, Detroit, Mich., 1969

Nead, L., 'The magdalen in modern times: the mythology of the fallen woman in Pre-Raphaelite painting', *Oxford art journal*, 7, i, 1984, p. 34; reprinted in R. Betterton, ed., *Looking on*, London, 1987, pp. 73–92

Nead, L., *Myths of sexuality. Representations of women in Victorian Britain*, Oxford, 1988

Nochlin, L., *Realism* (1973), 1987

Nochlin, L., 'The imaginary orient', *Art in America*, May 1983, pp. 119–91

Norton, S. and de Wolfe Howe, M.A., eds., *Letters of Charles Eliot Norton*, Boston, Mass. and New York, 1913

O'Neil, H. N., *Two thousand years hence*, London, 1868

Open University, *Religion: conformity and controversy/moral values and the social order*, A102 units 18–19/20–21, Milton Keynes, 1987

Parris, L. (ed.), *The Pre-Raphaelite papers*, London, 1984

Patmore, C., *The Poetical Works*, ed., F. Page, London and New York, 1949

Patmore, D., *The life and times of Coventry Patmore*, London, 1949

Philostratus, *Imagines*, trans. A. Fairbanks, London and Cambridge, Mass., 1960

Pliny the elder, *The elder Pliny's chapters on art*, trans. K. Jex-Blake, Chicago, Ill., 1976

Pratt, M. L., 'Fieldwork in common places' in J. Clifford, and G. E., Marcus, eds., *Writing culture*, Berkeley and Los Angeles, Ca., 1986

Preraffaelitak, Budapest: Magyar nemzeti galeria, 1979

A Pre-Raphaelite passion: the private collection of L. S. Lowry, Manchester, 1977

The Pre-Raphaelites, Tate Gallery, London, 1984

The Pre-Raphaelites and their circle in the National Gallery of Victoria, Melbourne, 1978

de Quincy, T., Confessions of an english opium eater and other writings, ed., G. Lindop, Oxford, 1985

Roberts, H., 'Marriage, redundancy or sin: the painter's view of women in the first twenty-five years of Victoria's reign' in M. Vicinus, ed., Suffer and be still, women in the Victorian age, Bloomington, Ind. (1972), 1980

Robinson, H. P., 'On combination printing', The photographic journal, 16 April 1860

Rose, A., Pre-Raphaelite portraits, Yeovil and Newbury Park, Ca., 1981

Rossetti, D. G., Family letters, W. M. Rossetti, ed., London, 1895

Rossetti, D. G., Preraphaelite diaries and letters, London, 1900

Rossetti, D. G., Some reminiscences, London, 1906

Rossetti, D. G., Letters of Dante Gabriel Rossetti, ed. O. Doughty and J. R. Wahl, Oxford, 1967

Rossetti, D. G., Rossetti–Morris correspondence, ed. J. Bryson and J. C. Troxell, Oxford, 1976

The Rossetti–Leyland letters: the correspondence of an artist and his patron, ed. F. Fennell, Athens, Ohio, 1978

Rossetti, W. M., Ruskin: Rossetti, PreRaphaelism. Papers, 1854–1862, London, 1899

Ruskin, J., The works of John Ruskin, ed. E. T. Cook and A. Wedderburn, London, 1903–12

Said, E., Orientalism (1978), Harmondsworth, 1985

Schneider, M., Neurosis and civilisation: a marxist/freudian synthesis, trans. M. Roloff, New York, 1975

Shaw-Sparrow, W., 'The collection of Mr. Alexander Henderson', Magazine of art, 1892, p. 20

Shefer, E., 'The nun and the convent in Pre-Raphaelite art', The journal of Pre-Raphaelite studies, 6, 2, May 1986, pp. 70–6

Spalding, R., Magnificent dreams: Burne-Jones and the late Victorians, New York, 1978

Spielman, M. H., Millais and his works, London, 1898

Stallybrass, P. and White A., 'Below stairs: the maid and the family romance', in The politics and poetics of transgression, Ithaca, NY and London, 1986

Stanford, D., ed., Pre-Raphaelite writing, London, 1973

Steinberg, L., The sexuality of Christ in renaissance art and modern oblivion, New York and Toronto, 1983

Stephens, F. G., William Holman Hunt and his works, London, 1860

Stevenson, R. A. M., 'Mr. Holman Hunt', anon. publication in Saturday review, LXI, 20, March 1886, p. 405

Surtees, V., The paintings and drawings of Dante Gabriel Rossetti (1828–1882) A catalogue raisonné, Oxford, 1971

Surtees, V., The correspondence and diaries of George Price Boyce, Norwich, 1980

Surtees, V., ed., The diaries of Ford Madox Brown, London, 1981

Tennyson: poems and plays, ed. T. H. Warren, London, 1975

The stereoscopic magazine: a gallery of landscape scenery, architecture, antiquities, and natural history, accompanied with descriptive articles by writers of eminence, London, 1858–65

Tilt, E. J., On the preservation of the health of women at the critical periods of life, London, 1851

Trevelyan, R., A Pre-Raphaelite circle, London, 1978

Vertrees, A., 'The picture making of Henry Peach Robinson' in D. Oliphant and T. Zigal, eds., Perspectives on photography, Austin, Texas, 1982

Warner, M., 'The professional career of John Everett Millais to 1863', Ph.D.,
    University of London, Courtauld Institute of Art, 1985

Warner, M., 'The question of faith: orientalism, Christianity and Islam' in *The
    orientalists: Delacroix to Matisse*, ed. M. A. Stevens, Royal Academy, London, 1984

Warner, Marina, *Monuments and maidens: the allegory of the female form*, London, 1985

Watts, Mary, ed., *George Frederick Watts*, London, 1912

Weeks, J., *The dream weavers: short stories by the nineteenth-century Pre-Raphaelite poet-
    painters*, Santa Barbara, Ca., 1980

Wheatsone, C., 'On some remarkable and hitherto unobserved phenomena of
    binocular vision', *Philosophical transactions of the Royal Society*, June 1838

Wheatstone, C., *The scientific papers of Sir Charles Wheatstone*, London, 1879

Wilkinson, Sir J. G., *The architecture of ancient Egypt . . . with remarks on the early progress of
    architecture, etc.*, London, 1850

Wilkinson, Sir J. G., *Modern Egypt and Thebes: being a description of Egypt, including the
    information required for travellers in that country*, 2 vols., London, 1843

Williams, R., 'The Bloomsbury fraction' in *Problems in materialism and culture*, London,
    1980, pp. 148–69

Wilson, H., 'The work of Edward Burne-Jones: more especially in decoration and
    design', *Architectural review*, 1, March 1897, p. 172

Wolff, J., *The social production of art*, London, 1981

Wood, C., *The Pre-Raphaelites*, New York, 1981

Wordsworth, W., *The poetical works of William Wordsworth*, ed. E. De Selincourt, edn,
    Oxford, 1952

Wordsworth, W., *The prelude: or growth of a poet's mind*, ed., E. De Selincourt, London,
    1933

Yeats, W. B., *Autobiographies*, London, 1955

Zipes, J., *Breaking the magic spell: radical theories of folk and fairy tales*, New York, 1979

Zipes, J. *Victorian fairy-tales: the revolt of the fairies and elves*, New York and London, 1987

Zipes, J., 'Setting standards for civilisation through fairy tales: Charles Perrault and
    his associates', *Fairy tales and the art of subversion*, New York, 1983

Newspapers and journals

Architectural review
Art journal
The *Athenaeum*
Contemporary review
Cornhill magazine
Daily News
The Germ: the literary magazine of the Pre-Raphaelites
The Globe
History workshop journal
Illustrated London news
Journal of Pre-Raphaelite Studies
Magazine of art
The magdalen's friend and female homes intelligencer
Morning chronicle

New monthly magazine
Pre-Raphaelite review
Saturday review
The Spectator
The stereoscopic magazine: a gallery of landscape scenery, architecture, antiquities, and natural history, accompanied with descriptive articles by writers of eminence
The Times
The Times literary supplement
Victorian studies

Notes on contributors

Marcia Pointon is Reader in History of Art at the University of Sussex where she has taught since 1975. She has published extensively in the field of British and European nineteenth-century art. Her Milton and English art (1970) was a pioneer interdisciplinary study. Two monographs, William Dyce, R.A. 1806–64: a critical biography (1979) and Mulready (1986) have contributed significantly to knowledge of major Victorian artists. Her work on Anglo-French artistic relations has been concerned with the social and cultural history of a trans-national stratum of artistic production in the first half of the nineteenth century. Bonington, Francia and Wyld and The Bonington circle: English watercolour and Anglo-French landscape were published in 1985. In addition to writing many articles for journals of art history, feminist studies, social history and Victorian studies, she is author of a widely used textbook, History of art: a students' handbook (1980, revised 1986).

Laura Marcus is Lecturer in English at the Polytechnic of Central London. She has written articles on and is researching in the area of nineteenth and twentieth-century autobiography.

Kate Flint, Fellow and Tutor in English at Mansfield College, Oxford, has published Dickens (1986) and edited Impressionism in England (1984) and The Victorian novelist: social problems and social change (1987). She is currently working on a study of the nineteenth-century woman reader.

Paul Barlow lectures in History of Art at Manchester Polytechnic and for the Open University; he is engaged in research into mid-nineteenth-century British painting.

Lindsay Smith is Lecturer in English at the University of Sussex. She is currently working on visual perception and optical agency in literature and painting.

Larry D. Lutchmansingh is Associate Professor of Art History at Bowdoin College, Brunswick, Me., USA. His research is centred primarily on late Victorian art, and he is currently engaged in a study on the Arts and Crafts Movement.

Lewis Johnson studied English at Cambridge and Art History at the University of Sussex. He is author of Prospects, thresholds, interiors: British watercolours from the Victoria and Albert Museum (forthcoming exhibition) and is researching into the rhetoric of visual communication, the comparisons and differences between images and language.

Index